THE NEW CLARENDON SHAKESPEARE

MACBETH

Edited by

BERNARD GROOM

Formerly Senior English Master
Clifton College

OXFORD
AT THE CLARENDON PRESS

Oxford University Press, Walton Street, Oxford OX2 6DP

OXFORD LONDON GLASGOW
NEW YORK TORONTO MELBOURNE WELLINGTON
KUALA LUMPUR SINGAPORE JAKARTA HONG KONG TOKYO
DELHI BOMBAY CALCUTTA MADRAS KARACHI
NAIROBI DAR ES SALAAM CAPE TOWN

© Oxford University Press 1939

First published 1939
Reprinted 1941, (with corrections), 1946, 1947, 1949, 1952,
1954, 1957, 1959, 1961, 1962, 1966, 1969, 1970, 1972, 1973
1974, 1975, 1977, 1978, 1979

THE NEW CLARENDON SHAKESPEARE

Under the general editorship of R. E. C. HOUGHTON, M.A.

Sometime Fellow, St. Peter's College, Oxford

	Edited by
Antony and Cleopatra	R. E. C. Houghton
As You Like It	Isabel J. Bisson
Coriolanus	B. H. Kemball-Cook
Hamlet	George Rylands
Henry IV, Part I	Bertram Newman
Henry IV, Part II	William R. Rutland
Henry V	Ronald F. W. Fletcher
Julius Caesar	R. E. C. Houghton
King Lear	R. E. C. Houghton
Macbeth	Bernard Groom
Measure for Measure	R. E. C. Houghton
Merchant of Venice	Ronald F. W. Fletcher
Midsummer Night's Dream	F. C. Horwood
Much Ado about Nothing	Philip Wayne
Othello	F. C. Horwood and R. E. C. Houghton
Richard II	John M. Lothian
Richard III	R. E. C. Houghton
Romeo and Juliet	R. E. C. Houghton
The Tempest	J. R. Sutherland
The Winter's Tale	S. L. Bethell
Twelfth Night	J. C. Dent

Printed in Hong Kong by Brighter Printing Press Ltd.

GENERAL PREFACE

THIS edition of Shakespeare aims primarily at presenting
the text in such a way that it can be easily read and understood. The language of Shakespeare presents considerable
difficulties to the beginner, difficulties which are soon forgotten and overlooked by readers who are familiar with the
plays. The answers of examination candidates often reveal
unexpected ignorance of quite ordinary Shakespearian
phraseology and vocabulary. In the notes, therefore, the
main emphasis has been placed on the interpretation of
words and phrases. Textual and linguistic matter, to
which much space was given in the old Clarendon Press
editions of Wright and Clark, has been kept in the background, but explanation is prominent. The notes have
been divided; words and phrases capable of a short explanation are glossed at the foot of the page, while the more
difficult passages are treated after the text in the general
commentary.

In the commentary alternative explanations and the
mention of critics by name have been avoided as far as
possible; on the other hand, there are a number of less
elementary notes on textual points and other matters not
strictly necessary for younger students, and these appear
in smaller type and within square brackets.

After the commentary is printed a substantial selection
from the best criticism of the play, old and new; a feature
in which this edition of Shakespeare follows the plan set by
the Clarendon English series. Here some matter will be
found suitable for more advanced students; and the in-
clusion of varying opinions will provide material for reflection and comparison. It is the editor's belief that students
can best be taught to criticize by the provision of material
which they may use as a starting-point as well as a model.

ACKNOWLEDGEMENTS

ACKNOWLEDGEMENT of permission to reprint copyright passages of literary criticism is gratefully made to:—Messrs. Macmillan & Co., Ltd. (A. C. Bradley, *Shakespearean Tragedy*); the representatives of the Rev. Stopford Brooke and Messrs. Constable & Co., Ltd. (*On Ten Plays of Shakespeare*); the Syndics of the Cambridge University Press (Sir A. T. Quiller-Couch, *Shakespeare's Workmanship*; Miss C. F. E. Spurgeon, *Shakespeare's Imagery*); the Oxford University Press (Robert Bridges, *The Influence of the Audience on Shakespeare's Drama*).

For the suggestions made in the section on the Shakespearian stage the editor is largely indebted to some notes kindly furnished by Mr. C. M. Haines, who is, however, not responsible for any errors that may have been introduced.

The text of Macbeth *here printed is complete except for the omission of one prose passage.*

CONTENTS

LIST OF PLATES

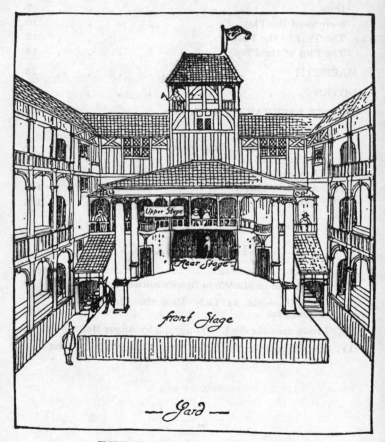

Upper Stage

Rear Stage

front Stage

— Yard —

THE FORTUNE THEATRE

A reconstruction by Mr. W. H. Godfrey from the builder's contract, which has survived. The theatre was built in 1600, two years later than the Globe, at which most of Shakespeare's plays were performed, and burnt down in 1621.

INTRODUCTION

DATE

THIS short introduction to *Macbeth* does not deal with its
dramatic qualities, which can scarcely escape any normal
reader or spectator. But when one has already read or
seen on the stage a play by Shakespeare, it is natural to ask,
sooner or later, certain questions about it. Was the play
written at the beginning, middle, or end of the dramatist's
career? Did he invent the plot, or was he indebted for any
part of it to some other writer? Further questions arise
in time; but these two are unavoidable, and hence one is
led to the problem of date and sources. Above all things a
practical dramatist, Shakespeare was not concerned to inform later generations in what year his plays were composed or first produced. But close study by lovers of Shakespeare has shown that approximate knowledge on this point
is generally possible. Two kinds of evidence have been
used to solve the problem. In the first place, plays which
are themselves undated nearly always have relations with
facts or events which are datable; this is external evidence.
Secondly, the variations in the style of the plays would be
utterly inexplicable if we did not assume that Shakespeare's
dramatic and poetic art went through various stages of
development; this being granted, we can arrange the plays
in a certain order according to their style and general
character; this is internal evidence.

To apply the second kind of evidence with precision
demands some technical knowledge of Shakespeare's style;
in particular, of his versification. This last point is briefly
dealt with in the Appendix (pp. 178–83). But, speaking
generally, one may affirm that *Macbeth* clearly belongs to
the period of the 'great tragedies'. By its merits and its
tragic character it is in the same class as *Hamlet, Othello,*

and *King Lear*; and, when added to these, it completes the
quartet of masterpieces which are Shakespeare's chief title
to fame. In its style, too, it belongs to this group, though
it was probably the last of the four to be written. The
qualities of the verse make this an almost certain conclusion. At all times of his life Shakespeare could write beautiful and melodious verse; but whereas his early verse is
slightly monotonous from its regularity, his latest verse is
as daring and varied as it can be, short of the total sacrifice
of all formal pattern. Now the verse of *Macbeth* is much
more free and bold than that of an early play like *A Mid-
summer Night's Dream*, but it is somewhat more formal
than that of a very late play like *The Winter's Tale*. Briefly,
the verse-tests place *Macbeth* last in order among the four
great tragedies, but before the plays of the 'final' period,
e.g. *Antony and Cleopatra*, *The Winter's Tale*, *The Tempest*,
and *Henry VIII*.

In examining the other evidence for the date, we notice
two outstanding facts which give us an early and a late
limit between which the date of the play must fall. *Macbeth* is clearly a compliment to the House of Stuart; its
general colouring is Scottish, there is an allusion to James I's
accession, and witchcraft—so prominent a feature of the
play—was a subject on which the new King regarded himself as an authority, and had even written a tract. *Macbeth* must, therefore, have been written after 1603, the date
of James's accession. On the other hand, there is a reference in the diary or note-book of a certain physician, Dr.
Simon Forman, to a performance of *Macbeth* which he had
seen on 20 April 1611. The date, therefore, lies between
the years 1603 and 1611. Other pieces of evidence help to
narrow the issue. One of these is a passage in a play called
The Puritan by one of Shakespeare's fellow dramatists,
Thomas Middleton. A character in this work observes:
'Instead of a jester, we'll ha' th' ghost in a white sheet sit

at upper end o' th' table.' Now the omission of a jester from *Macbeth* was a departure from Shakespeare's usual practice; moreover, Banquo's ghost sits in Macbeth's place: this, then, looks like a pointed allusion to Act III, Scene iv of the play, and if it is so, *Macbeth* must have been written before 1607, the year in which *The Puritan* was published. Clues to the date of a play are often given by the common practice of the time of alluding to noteworthy events or recent 'portents'. Two such allusions occur in the speech of the Porter (Act II, Sc. iii). The mention of 'an equivocator that could swear . . . against either scale; who committed treason enough for God's sake, yet could not equivocate to heaven' (ll. 8–11) is generally held to be an echo from the trial of the Jesuit Henry Garnet for complicity in the Gunpowder Plot: his defence of equivocation before the judges attracted much attention. The trial took place in March 1606, so it would seem that the play was written shortly after this time, otherwise the allusion would be out of date. Again, there may be a topical allusion in the sentence about the 'farmer that hanged himself on the expectation of plenty' (II. iii. 4–5). It has been shown that the harvest of 1606 was abundant, and that the price of corn in that year was considerably lower than in 1605 and 1607—a bad thing for farmers. Although allusions of this kind *might* have been inserted after the first composition of the play, they tend to support 1606 as the date of *Macbeth*. This conclusion harmonizes with the result suggested by the character and style of the play, for on that evidence we should be led to place *Macbeth* after *King Lear*, the date of which appears to be 1605–6. One other piece of historical evidence remains to be mentioned. The accession of James I aroused a certain interest in Scottish history among Englishmen, and the name of Banquo, the reputed ancestor of the Stuarts, was well known during the first years of the reign. In 1605 James visited Oxford, and we learn from a book called *Rex Platonicus* 'that on entering the city the King was addressed by three students of St. John's College, who alternately accosted his majesty, reciting some Latin verses, founded on the prediction of the weird sisters relative to Banquo and Macbeth' (Malone). Here is clear evidence of the interest which the Macbeth story was exciting in 1605. A popular dramatist like Shakespeare would naturally choose this period for producing his tragedy. Decisive proof is wanting, but with some confidence we may assign *Macbeth* to the year 1606, or perhaps, if the allusions in the Porter's speech are regarded as later insertions, to 1605; in any case to 1605–6.

THE SOURCES OF THE PLAY

Shakespeare did not invent the entire plots of his plays, and with good reason. An audience which knows beforehand the outline of a plot is more free to enjoy the pure drama of the situations; one which is puzzled to know 'what is happening' cannot be quickly responsive to the dramatist's art. *Macbeth* is a 'tragedy', but it is also a play on Scottish history, and like the series of English historical plays it is founded on the work of a writer well known to English readers, and invaluable to Shakespeare, Raphael Holinshed.

Holinshed's *Chronicles* were a compilation from the work of other writers. For the part dealing with Scottish affairs, Holinshed relied on the translation made in 1536 by John Bellenden of a Latin work entitled *Historia*, by Hector Boece. The work of Boece in its turn is founded on the works of John Fordun and Andrew Wyntoun, both of them writers of the fourteenth century. The events recorded in *Macbeth* must not be regarded as historical, nor are they purely imaginary; and what is very nearly a version of the tragedy in skeleton form may be found under the heading 'Macbeth' in the *Concise Dictionary of*

National Biography: 'Macbeth (d. 1057), King of Scotland;
commander of the forces of Duncan, King of Scotland,
whom he slew, and whose kingdom he took, 1040; defeated by Siward, earl of Northumbria, 1054; defeated and
slain by Malcolm III, Canmore, 1057.'

The remoteness and obscurity of the historical period
enabled Shakespeare to treat with great freedom the Macbeth story as told by Holinshed. His object was to write
a tragedy, not a 'chronicle-play', and by refashioning
characters and shifting incidents he is able to obtain much
finer dramatic effects than mere accuracy could produce.
To mention all his liberties with Holinshed would be
tedious: a few specimen instances will illustrate his purpose
and method. First, he obtains an effect of dramatic contrast by making Duncan better and Macbeth worse than
they are in the *Chronicles*. In the play, Duncan is the
picture of gracious majesty; in the *Chronicles*, he is a
weakling, excessively 'soft and gentle'. On the other hand,
Holinshed's Macbeth, though cruel and latterly tyrannical,
has ten years of good rule to his credit. Again, in the
Chronicles, Lady Macbeth is 'verie ambitious, burning in
unquenchable desire to beare the name of a queene'; in
Shakespeare, any hope she may have of her own aggrandise-
ment is swallowed up by her passionate desire for her husband's greatness. Equally remarkable is the way in which
Shakespeare has enriched the Macbeth story in Holinshed by combining it with another story from the same
source—also an account of a murder in the Royal House
of Scotland. Somewhat earlier in the *Chronicles* than the
Duncan-Macbeth story is an account of the murder of
King Duff by Donwald, and from here Shakespeare has
borrowed some of the most effective details of his play.
The following are examples: (1) Duff is murdered by
Donwald in the 'Castell of Fores', 'for the king being in
that countrie, was accustomed to be most commonlie

within the same castell, having a speciall trust in Donwald'
(cf. I. vii. 12–16). (2) Donwald 'abhorred the act greatlie
in his heart', but committed it 'through instigation of his
wife', who 'shewed him the meanes wherby he might
soonest accomplish it' (cf. I. vii). (3) When the king's
death is discovered, Donwald rushed into the chamber,
where 'he forthwith slue the chamberleins, as guiltie of
that heinous murther'; and afterwards 'he burdened the
chamberleins, whom he had slaine, with all the fault'
(cf. II. iii). (4) The alarming portents of the night on which
Duncan is killed are also suggested by the Donwald story:
'monstrous sights were seene' writes Holinshed; for
example, 'horsses in Louthian, being of singular beautie
and swiftnesse, did eate their own flesh' (cf. II. iv). Hence,
Shakespeare may be said to have used Holinshed's
Chronicles as a quarry from which to dig the materials
for his drama, rather than as an authority to be followed
in detail.

TEXT OF THE PLAY

Many of Shakespeare's plays were printed during his
lifetime, but twenty were not, and *Macbeth* is one of these.
It first appeared in 1623, in the edition of the plays prepared by two of his 'friends and fellows', John Heminge
and Henry Condell. This book has since been called the
First Folio—'folio' from its size and shape, 'first', because
other folio editions of the collected plays were published
from time to time. It is certain that Shakespeare's plays
as first printed often contained alterations of the author's
original draft and also printer's errors. The First Folio
seems to be founded on stage-versions of the plays rather
than on the poet's own manuscript. Some of the plays
were certainly adapted to suit the needs of the stage and
the demands of fashion. It would therefore not be surprising if the text of *Macbeth* as we have it in the Folio differed

somewhat from what Shakespeare originally wrote. This possibility has given rise to various speculations. The shortness of the play (it is the next shortest after *The Comedy of Errors*) has led some critics to suppose that the original version was longer—a suggestion which may be discussed but cannot be proved. Others think that passages have been added. On this point some extravagant views have been held,[1] but even the most sober critic may, I think, suspect that the 'Hecate-passages' (III. v. and IV. i. 39–43) were added after the first composition of the play (see Notes, p. 134). Another ground for suspecting that the text of the Folio has been tampered with is the inconsistency of the stage-directions in Act v. vii. Modern editions of the play correct an obvious error: but according to the Folio text the fighting in which Macbeth is killed takes place on the stage, though the direction at v. vii. 82, 'Enter Macduffe; with Macbeth's head', still stands. One may suppose that Shakespeare's intention of having Macbeth killed off the stage had been (imperfectly) altered in order to show the audience his duel with Macduff. This last example seems a clear proof that the text of the First Folio is not in every detail the authentic work of Shakespeare. Yet, when all is said, these are minute points, and for suspecting that they imply any corruption of the text on a large scale there is really no ground at all. Most of the points at which a modern edition departs from the Folio in this play are corrections of obvious mistakes, e.g. 'martlet' for 'barlet' (I. vi. 4); 'strides' for 'sides' (II. i. 55).

This edition follows the Oxford text except in III. ii. 42, where 'shard-born' has been substituted for 'shard-borne' on the authority of the *O.E.D.* The punctuation of the Oxford text has not always been followed.

---

[1] e.g. Mr. Henry Cunningham, editor of *Macbeth* in 'The Arden Shakespeare' dismisses Act I, Sc. ii, as 'most certainly spurious'.

MACBETH ON THE SHAKESPEARIAN STAGE

The Elizabethan theatre was a very different affair from the modern one. The latter, a 'picture stage', in which the audience may be said to constitute the 'fourth wall' of a room, aims at illusion; the former, in which the stage was a platform thrust out among an audience, could not hope for this. A glance at the illustration will make a long explanation unnecessary. The platform constitutes the front or main stage; entrance was at the back (through any of several doors), not at the sides, so that some time elapsed between a character's appearance and his reaching the front of the stage. The building at the rear had a gallery above, which served for walls of a city, balcony of a room, &c. Below were curtains which, when drawn back, served to provide a *rear* or *inner stage*. As there were no means of closing the outer stage, scenes which had to be disclosed or hidden took place on this inner stage. There was little approximation to scenery, but plenty of movable properties (e.g. a 'mossy bank'). There was also a trap-door for the removal of properties, and for certain stage effects.

Our knowledge of the precise uses to which the various parts of the stage were put is far from perfect, and we know still less of the conventions which an Elizabethan audience was prepared to accept. Devices which would provoke amusement in a London theatre of to-day were probably accepted as a matter of course by the simpler-minded Elizabethans. Some of Shakespeare's plays are quite easy to imagine on the stage of the time, but *Macbeth* presents a number of difficult problems. The following suggestions are necessarily based to a large extent on conjecture.

In general, the full stage (with curtains open) was used very little in *Macbeth*, partly perhaps to add to the effect of rapidity and directness of attack. The Witches present a peculiarly difficult problem. Act I, Scene i, was probably played on the front stage. In Act I, Scene iii, the Witches probably meet Macbeth and Banquo on the front stage: they have no cauldron or other properties here to make this difficult, and l. 77 suggests that they meet the two men on their way across the (front) stage. How they vanish at the next line no one can satisfactorily explain. They could, of course, pass through the (closed) curtains, or if these were open, they might move on to the inner stage and be concealed by the closing of the curtains. But if anything so obvious as either of these devices was used, lines 80 and 81 might be apt to sound ridiculous. (It is possible, however, that to an audience of James I's time, witches were so terrifying a reality that nothing they might do was in any danger of raising a laugh.) The phrase 'into the air' (l. 81) suggests that they cannot have disappeared through the trap-door.

In Act III, Scene iv, the full stage was undoubtedly used. The curtains are open, and the banquet is prepared on the inner stage. At l. 8 the First Murderer enters, and at l. 12, Macbeth comes forward to meet him. (The stage-direction in F. is 'Approaching in the door'.) Their colloquy takes place on the front stage. Macbeth is recalled to the banquet by Lennox at l. 39, but it seems that he hovers between the front and inner stages until l. 88, when he seats himself at the banquet. At l. 58, Lady Macbeth leaves the inner stage, and the dialogue with her husband (ll. 58–84) takes place on the front stage. For a short time (ll. 84–121) the action takes place on the inner stage, but when the guests have departed, Macbeth and Lady Macbeth no doubt come forward, and the scene is concluded on the front stage.

Act IV, Scene i, opens with the inner stage representing the cavern. At l. 48 Macbeth enters on the front stage. So much is clear; the rest of the scene is rather difficult to reconstruct. It might appear at first sight that the gallery or upper stage was used for the raising of the Apparitions. But l. 74 suggests that as Macbeth starts towards the first Apparition, his way is barred by the First Witch, who is now with Macbeth on the front stage. Again, the rising and sinking of the Apparitions would be ineffective behind the railings of the upper stage. Most likely the trap-door—the regular device for magical effects—was used for the Apparitions. Hence the word 'descends' (IV. i. 72, 81, 94), which is seldom used for an exit from the upper stage. When the Apparitions have vanished, the cauldron also descends (l. 106), to make room for the Show of Kings, who probably walk on at one side of the inner stage and stand in a row across it. It is possible that they, like the Apparitions, come up through the trap-door (cf. Macbeth's 'down!' at l. 112); but this seems doubtful, as it would be a cumbrous way of bringing nine people on to the stage, and the effect would be lost by iteration.

In Act v, the inner stage was probably used in Scenes iv and vi. In Scene iv it serves as the wood of Birnam; or, to speak in terms of practical necessity, the place from which the soldiers collect their boughs. Presumably they walk off the stage with the boughs, and reappear carrying them in Scene vi. Here, the inner stage serves as the place where the boughs are deposited, after the Army has entered in the manner described in the stage-direction.

THE PLOT

I. i. The Tragedy opens amid thunder and lightning. Three Witches agree to meet Macbeth at the close of a battle which is now raging.

I. ii. Tidings of the battle are brought to Duncan, King of Scotland. He learns that his cousin Macbeth, thane of Glamis, has killed the rebel Macdonwald, and in a second conflict has defeated Macdonwald's Norwegian allies, and the traitorous thane of Cawdor. Duncan decides to confer Cawdor's title on the victorious Macbeth, and sends Ross to convey the honour.

I. iii. The witches are met by the two captains of Duncan's army. They greet Macbeth by three titles, thane of Glamis, thane of Cawdor, and 'king hereafter'. The other captain, Banquo, receives the promise that, though no king himself, he shall be the father of kings. Ross then arrives, and salutes Macbeth as 'thane of Cawdor'. This sudden fulfilment of one prophecy turns Macbeth's mind forcibly on the promise of kingship, and he expresses his thought of murdering Duncan to gain this throne in the muttered words of an aside. With an effort he brings his mind back to the present situation.

I. iv. The aged king meets his cousin and captain with a heart full of gratitude. He creates Malcolm, his elder son, Prince of Cumberland, and declares his intention of following Macbeth to Inverness as his guest.

I. v. The scene shifts to Inverness: Lady Macbeth is reading of the witches' prophecy in a letter from her husband. She knows his ambition, and she knows his scruples; it is her part to inflame the one, and to remove the other. She steels herself for the effort, and on her husband's entrance, assures him in a few words of her support in the 'great business' now impending.

I. vi. Following on the heels of Macbeth, Duncan and Banquo enter the castle at Inverness, and are graciously welcomed by their hostess.

I. vii. A banquet is in progress on the same night. Macbeth has slipped away from his guests, and sees with fearful clearness the horror of his projected crime. He resolves to 'proceed no further'. But his wife has now joined him, and with a supreme effort of persuasion she brings him back to his first intention. Leaving no time for further hesitation, she promises her own help. She will make drunk with wine the two grooms of the chamber who protect the king, and after the deed will smear their faces with blood and so cast on them suspicion of the murder.

II. i. The moment for the deed is at hand. After a short dialogue with Banquo, Macbeth is left alone in suspense, awaiting the sound of the bell which is to be the signal for action (ll. 62–4).

II. ii. A few minutes have elapsed. Lady Macbeth is waiting breathlessly for sounds from Duncan's chamber. Macbeth enters, distraught and terror-stricken. He has mistakenly brought with him the blood-stained daggers which should have been left by the sleeping grooms. Suddenly a noise of knocking is heard. With a great effort Lady Macbeth recalls her husband to the needs of the moment.

II. iii. The knocking has come from Macduff and Lennox, early arrivals at the Castle. Macduff enters Duncan's chamber, and almost instantly returns with the news of his death. Confusion follows. Macbeth leaves the stage, and on his return announces that he has killed the grooms in a fit of rage. The two young princes, scenting treachery, agree to flee the country: Malcolm will take refuge in England, Donalbain in Ireland.

II. iv. An old man describes to Ross the strange portents seen on the night of Duncan's murder. Macduff enters and informs Ross that suspicion has fallen on the fugitive princes, and that Macbeth has gone to Scone to be invested as king.

III. i. An interval has elapsed, and Macbeth is now king. The prophecy of the Witches that the royal line should descend not from Macbeth but from Banquo is now uppermost in the minds of both men. Macbeth elicits from Banquo particulars of his own and of his son's movements, and rapidly plans their joint murder. The execution of the crime is entrusted to two hired cut-throats, and it is to be performed on the same night, at some distance from the palace.

III. ii. This short scene does not carry on the action, but it shows the changed relations between Macbeth and his wife. Lady Macbeth's object now is to soothe her husband's mind as far as she can, and to shut her eyes to his actions.

III. iii. The two murderers, joined by a third, await the approach of Banquo and Fleance. Banquo is killed, but Fleance escapes.

III. iv. A banquet, to which Banquo has been invited, is in progress on the night of his murder. News is brought to Macbeth that his attempt has partly succeeded, and partly failed. The banquet proceeds, and the ghost of Banquo, visible only to Macbeth, seats itself in the vacant place. The king's terror and agony cannot be concealed from his guests, and the company is broken up. Macbeth now informs the queen that Macduff is holding aloof from the Court, and that he suspects the loyalty of other nobles. He declares his intention of visiting the Witches to learn the worst that is in store for him.

III. v. Hecate warns the other witches that Macbeth will shortly visit them to learn his destiny.

III. vi. A dialogue between Lennox and another lord indicating the universal suspicion and fear which Macbeth's actions have at length aroused in Scotland. Macduff has joined Malcolm at the English Court and hopes to obtain the help of Edward the Confessor against 'the tyrant'.

IV. i. A cavern is disclosed where the three Witches are uttering incantations around a boiling cauldron. They command Macbeth to beware of Macduff, but to fear harm from no man born of woman; and they declare that he shall never be vanquished until Birnam Wood shall come to Dunsinane Hill (for the Apparitions, see note on p. 136). Though warned to seek no more, he insists on learning whether Banquo's issue shall reign in Scotland; whereupon a vision is raised of the Stuart kings in long succession, showing by their features their descent from Banquo. The scene ends with the news that Macduff has fled to England; Macbeth swears to surprise his castle and destroy his family.

IV. ii. The threat is executed. Lady Macduff and her little son are confronted by two Murderers, and the boy is killed before his mother's eyes.

IV. iii. An interval may be assumed. Malcolm, a refugee in England, knows so well the treachery of Macbeth that the arrival of Macduff, who has left his family in 'the tyrant's' power, fills him with suspicion. To test his loyalty, he accuses himself of imaginary crimes, until the apparent wreck of Scotland's last hope of a good king provokes Macduff to an outburst of patriotic despair which can leave no doubt. The explanation is barely ended before Ross arrives with the news of the utter destruction of Macduff's family. Macduff's first feelings of grief harden into a vehement resolve for vengeance.

V. i. Lady Macbeth has long lost her power over her husband's actions, but she has kept her own capacity for suffering, and what she has suffered in secret is revealed in the scene of her sleep-walking.

V. ii. Another interval. The Scottish insurgents are on their march towards Birnam to meet their allies from England.

V. iii. Macbeth fortifies himself at Dunsinane with a mixture of desperation and defiance.

V. iv. Malcolm, near Dunsinane, orders his soldiers to bear before them boughs cut from Birnam Wood, in order to 'shadow the numbers' of the host.

V. v. Macbeth learns that his wife is dead. The report that Birnam Wood has in appearance begun to move rouses him to a frenzy of anger.

V. vi. Malcolm directs the two Siwards, father and son,

to command one division of the army; himself and Macduff command the other.

V. vii. Macbeth kills young Siward on the battle-field. Malcolm's army meets little resistance, and the Castle of Dunsinane is surrendered. Macbeth meets Macduff, confident in the thought that he is invulnerable 'by one of woman born'. Macduff answers that he was not, in the usual sense, *born*, but 'was from his mother's womb Untimely ripp'd'. The combatants leave the stage, fighting. Shortly after Macduff enters with Macbeth's head, and the assembled nobles salute Malcolm as 'King of Scotland'.

DRAMATIS PERSONAE

DUNCAN, King of Scotland.

MALCOLM,
DONALBAIN, } his Sons.

MACBETH,
BANQUO, } Generals of the King's Army.

MACDUFF,
LENNOX,
ROSS,
MENTEITH, } Noblemen of Scotland.
ANGUS,
CAITHNESS,

FLEANCE, Son to Banquo.
SIWARD, Earl of Northumberland, General of the English Forces.
YOUNG SIWARD, his Son.
SEYTON, an Officer attending Macbeth.
Boy, Son to Macduff.
An English Doctor.
A Scotch Doctor.
A Sergeant.
A Porter.
An Old Man.

LADY MACBETH.
LADY MACDUFF.
Gentlewoman attending on Lady Macbeth.

HECATE and Three Witches.

Lords, Gentlemen, Officers, Soldiers, Murderers, Attendants, and
    Messengers. The Ghost of Banquo, and other Apparitions.

SCENE.—*Scotland; England.*

MACBETH

ACT I

Scene I. A DESERT HEATH

Thunder and lightning. Enter three Witches.

First Witch. When shall we three meet again
In thunder, lightning, or in rain?
Second Witch. When the hurlyburly's done,
When the battle's lost and won.
Third Witch. That will be ere the set of sun.   5
First Witch. Where the place?
Second Witch.   Upon the heath.
Third Witch. There to meet with Macbeth.
First Witch. I come, Graymalkin!
Second Witch. Paddock calls.
Third Witch. Anon.   10
All. Fair is foul, and foul is fair:
Hover through the fog and filthy air.   [*Exeunt.*

Scene II. A CAMP NEAR FORRES

Alarum within. Enter KING DUNCAN, MALCOLM,
DONALBAIN, LENNOX, *with* Attendants, *meeting a*
bleeding Sergeant.

Duncan. What bloody man is that? He can report,
As seemeth by his plight, of the revolt
The newest state.

Glossarial notes dealing with words and phrases, and paraphrases
of difficult passages, are given at the foot of the page where such seem
necessary to keep the sense running. Other notes are printed in the
commentary at the end. The sign [N] in the footnotes indicates that a
further note on the same line will be found in the commentary.

3 hurlyburly: the din and tumult of battle.   **10 Anon:** I'm
coming. (Literally, at once, in a moment.)

Malcolm.   This is the sergeant
Who, like a good and hardy soldier, fought
'Gainst my captivity. Hail, brave friend!   5
Say to the king the knowledge of the broil
As thou didst leave it.

   Sergeant.   Doubtful it stood;
As two spent swimmers, that do cling together
And choke their art. The merciless Macdonwald—
Worthy to be a rebel, for to that   10
The multiplying villanies of nature
Do swarm upon him—from the western isles
Of kerns and gallowglasses is supplied;
And fortune, on his damned quarrel smiling,
Show'd like a rebel's whore: but all's too weak;   15
For brave Macbeth,—well he deserves that name,—
Disdaining fortune, with his brandish'd steel,
Which smok'd with bloody execution,
Like valour's minion carv'd out his passage
Till he fac'd the slave;   20
Which ne'er shook hands, nor bade farewell to him,
Till he unseam'd him from the nave to the chaps,
And fix'd his head upon our battlements.

   Duncan. O valiant cousin! worthy gentleman!

   Sergeant. As whence the sun 'gins his reflection   25
Shipwracking storms and direful thunders break,

---

6 **the knowledge:** thy knowledge.   9 **choke their art:**
frustrate their own skill [*N*].   10 **to that:** to that end.   13
kerns and gallowglasses: respectively, light-armed and heavy-
armed troops from Ireland.   **of . . . is supplied:** is furnished
with.   14 **quarrel:** cause of dispute.   15 **Show'd . . .**
whore. Fortune appeared like the rebel's mistress, wearing a fickle
smile.   19 **minion:** darling, favourite.   21 **which:** i.e.
Macbeth [*N*].   **shook hands:** made a formal greeting (as before
a duel).   22 **unseam'd . . . chaps:** ripped him open from the
navel to the face.   25 **As . . . reflection:** as from the east....
26 **Shipwracking:** shipwrecking. Cf. I. iii. 29, 114, v. v. 51.

So from that spring whence comfort seem'd to come
Discomfort swells. Mark, King of Scotland, mark:
No sooner justice had with valour arm'd
Compell'd these skipping kerns to trust their heels,   30
But the Norweyan lord, surveying vantage,
With furbish'd arms and new supplies of men
Began a fresh assault.

Duncan.   Dismay'd not this
Our captains, Macbeth and Banquo?

Sergeant.   Yes;
As sparrows eagles, or the hare the lion.   35
If I say sooth, I must report they were
As cannons overcharg'd with double cracks;
So they
Doubly redoubled strokes upon the foe:
Except they meant to bathe in reeking wounds,   40
Or memorize another Golgotha,
I cannot tell—
But I am faint, my gashes cry for help.

Duncan. So well thy words become thee as thy wounds;
They smack of honour both. Go, get him surgeons.   45

        [*Exit* SERGEANT, *attended.*

Enter ROSS.

Who comes here?

Malcolm.   The worthy Thane of Ross.

Lennox. What a haste looks through his eyes! So should
  he look

27 **spring**: source.   28 **Discomfort**: disaster.   **swells**:
i.e. like a destructive river.   30 **skipping**: nimble (of light-
armed troops).   **kerns**: cf. I. ii. 13.   31 **surveying vantage**:
perceiving a favourable opportunity.   32 **furbish'd**: polished
up, fresh.   34 **Yes.** The next line proves his 'Yes' to be an
emphatic 'No'.   37 **cracks**: charges.   40 **except**: unless.
41 **memorize . . . Golgotha**: set up in men's memories another
'place of skulls' [*N*].   42 'I don't know how to describe what
they were doing.'   44 **So well**: as well.

That seems to speak things strange.

   Ross.   God save the king!

   Duncan. Whence cam'st thou, worthy thane?

   Ross.   From Fife, great king;

Where the Norweyan banners flout the sky   50

And fan our people cold. Norway himself,

With terrible numbers,

Assisted by that most disloyal traitor,

The Thane of Cawdor, began a dismal conflict;

Till that Bellona's bridegroom, lapp'd in proof,   55

Confronted him with self-comparisons,

Point against point, rebellious arm 'gainst arm,

Curbing his lavish spirit: and, to conclude,

The victory fell on us.—

   Duncan.   Great happiness!

   Ross. That now   60

Sweno, the Norways' king, craves composition;

Nor would we deign him burial of his men

Till he disbursed, at Saint Colme's Inch,

Ten thousand dollars to our general use.

   Duncan. No more that Thane of Cawdor shall deceive   65

Our bosom interest. Go pronounce his present death,

And with his former title greet Macbeth.

   Ross. I'll see it done.

   Duncan. What he hath lost noble Macbeth hath won.

                                  [Exeunt.

---

51 **fan . . . cold:** wave chilling fear into the hearts of our people.
Norway himself: the King of Norway.   55 **Bellona's
bridegroom:** i.e. Macbeth [*N*].   **lapp'd in proof:**
enclosed in impenetrable armour.   56 **Confronted . . . self-
comparisons:** faced him with warlike qualities which matched his
own.   57 **rebellious:** contending.   58 **lavish:** unrestrained,
outrageous.   60 **That:** so that. Cf. I. iii. 57, IV. iii. 82.   61
composition: terms.   66 **Our . . . interest:** my (from the
royal 'our') close affection (for him).   **present:** immediate.

Scene III. A Heath

Thunder. Enter the three Witches.

First Witch. Where hast thou been, sister?
Second Witch. Killing swine.
Third Witch. Sister, where thou?
First Witch. A sailor's wife had chestnuts in her lap,
And munch'd, and munch'd, and munch'd: 'Give me,'
    quoth I: 5
'Aroint thee, witch!' the rump-fed ronyon cries.
Her husband's to Aleppo gone, master o' the Tiger:
But in a sieve I'll thither sail,
And, like a rat without a tail,
I'll do, I'll do, and I'll do. 10
  Second Witch. I'll give thee a wind.
  First Witch. Thou'rt kind.
  Third Witch. And I another.
  First Witch. I myself have all the other;
And the very ports they blow, 15
All the quarters that they know
I' the shipman's card.
I'll drain him dry as hay:
Sleep shall neither night nor day
Hang upon his pent-house lid; 20
He shall live a man forbid.
Weary se'nnights nine times nine
Shall he dwindle, peak and pine:
Though his bark cannot be lost,
Yet it shall be tempest-tost. 25

6 **Aroint thee:** begone, avaunt. **rump-fed:** (probably) pampered, fed on the best joints. **ronyon:** 'an abusive term applied to a woman' (*O.E.D.*). 14 **other** is plural. Understand 'winds'. 15 **the . . . blow:** I can decide the ports they blow to. 17 **shipman's card:** the compass card. 20 **pent-house lid:** eyelid [*N*]. 21 **forbid:** shunned, banned. 22 **se'nnights:** weeks. 23 **peak:** waste away.

Look what I have.

 Second Witch. Show me, show me.

 First Witch. Here I have a pilot's thumb,
Wrack'd as homeward he did come.   *[Drum within.*

 Third Witch. A drum! a drum!   80
Macbeth doth come.

 All. The weird sisters, hand in hand,
Posters of the sea and land,
Thus do go about, about:
Thrice to thine, and thrice to mine,   35
And thrice again, to make up nine.
Peace! the charm's wound up.

Enter MACBETH *and* BANQUO.

 Macbeth. So foul and fair a day I have not seen.

 Banquo. How far is 't call'd to Forres? What are these,
So wither'd and so wild in their attire,   40
That look not like th' inhabitants o' the earth,
And yet are on 't? Live you? or are you aught
That man may question? You seem to understand me,
By each at once her choppy finger laying
Upon her skinny lips: you should be women, 45
And yet your beards forbid me to interpret
That you are so.

 Macbeth.   Speak, if you can: what are you?

 First Witch. All hail, Macbeth! hail to thee, Thane of
   Glamis!

 Second Witch. All hail, Macbeth! hail to thee, Thane of
   Cawdor!

 Third Witch. All hail, Macbeth! that shalt be king hereafter.   50

 Banquo. Good sir, why do you start, and seem to fear

29 **Wrack'd**: Cf. I. ii. 26. 32 **weird sisters**: sisters who control
destinies or 'weirds' [*N*]. 33 **Posters**: travellers. 44 **choppy**:
chapped. 45 **you . . . women**: you must surely be women.

Things that do sound so fair? I' the name of truth,
Are ye fantastical, or that indeed
Which outwardly ye show? My noble partner
You greet with present grace and great prediction   55
Of noble having and of royal hope,
That he seems rapt withal: to me you speak not.
If you can look into the seeds of time,
And say which grain will grow and which will not,
Speak then to me, who neither beg nor fear   60
Your favours nor your hate.

   First Witch. Hail!
   Second Witch. Hail!
   Third Witch. Hail!
   First Witch. Lesser than Macbeth, and greater.   65
   Second Witch. Not so happy, yet much happier.
   Third Witch. Thou shalt get kings, though thou be none:
So, all hail, Macbeth and Banquo!
   First Witch. Banquo and Macbeth, all hail!
   Macbeth. Stay, you imperfect speakers, tell me more: 70
By Sinel's death I know I am Thane of Glamis;
But how of Cawdor? the Thane of Cawdor lives,
A prosperous gentleman; and to be king
Stands not within the prospect of belief,
No more than to be Cawdor. Say from whence   75
You owe this strange intelligence? or why
Upon this blasted heath you stop our way
With such prophetic greeting? Speak, I charge you.

                            [Witches *vanish.*

---

53 fantastical: unreal, fancied.   **54 show:** appear.   **55
present grace,** i.e. the title (Thane of Glamis) which Macbeth already
possesses.   **56 noble having ... royal hope:** possession of noble
rank (i.e. the thaneship of Cawdor) ... hope of royalty.   **57 That:**
see note on I. ii. 60.   **60–1:** i.e. who neither beg your favours nor
fear your hate.   **67 get:** beget.   **70 imperfect:** because they
stop short.   **74–5:** is not more credible than to be Cawdor.
(Double negative.)   **76 owe:** possess.

Banquo. The earth hath bubbles, as the water has,
And these are of them. Whither are they vanish'd?   80
  Macbeth. Into the air, and what seem'd corporal melted
As breath into the wind. Would they had stay'd!
  Banquo. Were such things here as we do speak about?
Or have we eaten on the insane root
That takes the reason prisoner?   85
  Macbeth. Your children shall be kings.
  Banquo.   You shall be king.
  Macbeth. And Thane of Cawdor too; went it not so?
  Banquo. To the self-same tune and words. Who's here?

Enter ROSS *and* ANGUS.

  Ross. The king hath happily receiv'd, Macbeth,
The news of thy success; and when he reads   90
Thy personal venture in the rebels' fight,
His wonders and his praises do contend
Which should be thine or his. Silenc'd with that,
In viewing o'er the rest o' the self-same day,
He finds thee in the stout Norweyan ranks,   95
Nothing afeard of what thyself didst make,
Strange images of death. As thick as hail
Came post with post, and every one did bear
Thy praises in his kingdom's great defence,
And pour'd them down before him.
  Angus.   We are sent   100
To give thee from our royal master thanks;
Only to herald thee into his sight,
Not pay thee.

84 **on**: of.   **the insane root**: the root that produces insanity.
92–3 **His wonders . . . his.** Words are inadequate to the occasion;
hence the king is torn by a conflict of doubt whether 'his wonders'
should remain 'his' (by not being expressed), or his (imperfect)
praises should be bestowed on Macbeth.   98 **post with post**:
one messenger after another.

Ross. And, for an earnest of a greater honour,
He bade me, from him, call thee Thane of Cawdor: 105
In which addition, hail, most worthy thane!
For it is thine.

Banquo.   What! can the devil speak true?

Macb. The Thane of Cawdor lives: why do you dress me
In borrow'd robes?

Angus.   .   Who was the thane lives yet;
But under heavy judgment bears that life   110
Which he deserves to lose. Whether he was combin'd
With those of Norway, or did line the rebel
With hidden help or vantage, or that with both
He labour'd in his country's wrack, I know not;
But treasons capital, confess'd and prov'd,   115
Have overthrown him.

Macbeth. [*Aside.*] Glamis, and Thane of Cawdor:
The greatest is behind. [*To* ROSS *and* ANGUS.] Thanks for
     your pains.

[*To* BANQUO.] Do you not hope your children shall be
     kings,
When those that give the Thane of Cawdor to me
Promis'd no less to them?

Banquo.   That, trusted home,   120
Might yet enkindle you unto the crown,
Besides the Thane of Cawdor. But 'tis strange:
And oftentimes, to win us to our harm,
The instruments of darkness tell us truths,
Win us with honest trifles, to betray 's   125

104 **earnest**: pledge.   ·106 **addition**: title.   112 **line**:
reinforce.   114 **wrack**: wreck. See note I. ii. 26.   117
behind: to follow.   119 **Thane**: i.e. thaneship.   120 **That,
trusted home**: the prophecy, completely believed, complete belief in
the prophecy [*N*].   121 **enkindle you**: incite you to hope for.
125–6 **Win us . . . consequence**: they win our confidence by
true reports about trifles, so as to deceive us in matters of great
importance.

In deepest consequence.
Cousins, a word, I pray you.

   Macbeth. [*Aside.*]   Two truths are told,
As happy prologues to the swelling act
Of the imperial theme. I thank you, gentlemen.
[*Aside.*] This supernatural soliciting   130
Cannot be ill, cannot be good; if ill,
Why hath it given me earnest of success,
Commencing in a truth? I am Thane of Cawdor:
If good, why do I yield to that suggestion
Whose horrid image doth unfix my hair   135
And make my seated heart knock at my ribs,
Against the use of nature? Present fears
Are less than horrible imaginings;
My thought, whose murder yet is but fantastical,
Shakes so my single state of man that function   140
Is smother'd in surmise, and nothing is
But what is not.

   Banquo.   Look, how our partner's rapt.

   Macbeth. [*Aside.*] If chance will have me king, why,
     chance may crown me,
Without my stir.

   Banquo.   New honours come upon him,
Like our strange garments, cleave not to their mould 145

---

127 Cousins: a common term of friendship between sovereigns
and peers.   **128 swelling:** causing the heart to 'swell' with
emotion.   **129 imperial theme:** i.e. the rise of Macbeth to
kingship and empire.   **130 supernatural soliciting:** instigation
by supernatural beings.   **132 earnest:** pledge.   **134 suggestion:** temptation.   **136 seated:** (normally) fixed in place.
137 use: custom.   **139 My thought . . . fantastical:** my
thought, in which murder is yet only an imagination.   **140 single
state:** unity [*N*].   **function:** power of action.   **141 smother'd
in surmise:** lost in speculation.   **141–2 nothing . . . not:**
nothing is real to me but what I imagine.   **142 partner:** companion.   **144 come:** that have come.   **145 strange:** new,
unfamiliar.   **mould:** the form of the body.

But with the aid of use.
  Macbeth.   [*Aside.*] Come what come may,
Time and the hour runs through the roughest day.
  Banquo. Worthy Macbeth, we stay upon your leisure.
  Macb. Give me your favour: my dull brain was wrought
With things forgotten. Kind gentlemen, your pains   150
Are register'd where every day I turn
The leaf to read them. Let us toward the king.
Think upon what hath chanc'd; and, at more time,
The interim having weigh'd it, let us speak
Our free hearts each to other.
  Banquo.   Very gladly.   155
  Macbeth. Till then, enough. Come, friends.   [*Exeunt.*

Scene IV. FORRES. A ROOM IN THE PALACE

Flourish. Enter DUNCAN, MALCOLM, DONALBAIN,
LENNOX, *and* Attendants.

  Duncan. Is execution done on Cawdor? Are not
Those in commission yet return'd?
  Malcolm.   My liege,
They are not yet come back; but I have spoke
With one that saw him die; who did report
That very frankly he confess'd his treasons,   5
Implor'd your highness' pardon and set forth
A deep repentance. Nothing in his life
Became him like the leaving it; he died
As one that had been studied in his death
To throw away the dearest thing he ow'd,   10

147 **Time . . . day:** the most tempestuous day comes to an end
[*N*].   149 **wrought:** agitated.   153 **at more time:** at
leisure.   154 **The interim . . . it:** the interval having given
us time to weigh it.   154–5 **speak . . . hearts:** speak freely.
2 **Those in commission:** the persons appointed to execute Cawdor.
6 **set forth:** professed.   9 **As one . . . death:** as one who had
practised the art of dying (so as to).   10 **ow'd:** cf. I. iii. 76.

As 'twere a careless trifle.

Duncan.   There's no art
To find the mind's construction in the face:
He was a gentleman on whom I built
An absolute trust.

> *Enter* MACBETH, BANQUO, ROSS, *and* ANGUS.

                    O worthiest cousin!
The sin of my ingratitude even now   15
Was heavy on me. Thou art so far before
That swiftest wing of recompense is slow
To overtake thee; would thou hadst less deserv'd,
That the proportion both of thanks and payment
Might have been mine! only I have left to say,   20
More is thy due than more than all can pay.

Macbeth. The service and the loyalty I owe,
In doing it, pays itself. Your highness' part
Is to receive our duties; and our duties
Are to your throne and state, children and servants;   25
Which do but what they should, by doing everything
Safe toward your love and honour.

Duncan.   Welcome hither:
I have begun to plant thee, and will labour
To make thee full of growing. Noble Banquo,
That hast no less deserv'd, nor must be known   30

11 **careless trifle**: thing of no moment.   12 **There's no art . . . face**: there's no method of discovering the nature of a man's mind from his face.   17–8 **swiftest . . . thee**: the desire to reward you is outstripped by your merits.   19–20 **That . . . mine**: that my thanks and my payment might have been duly proportioned, i.e. that my power to reward you might have equalled my gratitude.   21 **all**: i.e. all I have, or, all I can give.   23 **In doing . . . itself**: loyal service is its own reward.   27 **Safe toward**: with a sure regard to.   28 **I have begun . . . thee**. The metaphor 'begun to plant thee' alludes to the granting of Cawdor's title, the first proof of Duncan's favour.   30–1 **nor . . . done so**: and must be no less known, &c.

No less to have done so, let me infold thee
And hold thee to my heart.
  Banquo.   There if I grow,
The harvest is your own.
  Duncan.   My plenteous joys
Wanton in fulness, seek to hide themselves
In drops of sorrow. Sons, kinsmen, thanes,   35
And you whose places are the nearest, know
We will establish our estate upon
Our eldest, Malcolm, whom we name hereafter
The Prince of Cumberland; which honour must
Not unaccompanied invest him only,   40
But signs of nobleness, like stars, shall shine
On all deservers. From hence to Inverness,
And bind us further to you.
  Macbeth. The rest is labour, which is not us'd for you:
I'll be myself the harbinger, and make joyful   45
The hearing of my wife with your approach;
So, humbly take my leave.
  Duncan.   My worthy Cawdor!
  Macbeth. [*Aside.*] The Prince of Cumberland! that is a
    step
On which I must fall down, or else o'er-leap,
For in my way it lies. Stars, hide your fires!   50
Let not light see my black and deep desires;
The eye wink at the hand; yet let that be
Which the eye fears, when it is done, to see.   [*Exit.*
  Duncan. True, worthy Banquo; he is full so valiant,
And in his commendations I am fed;   55
It is a-banquet to me. Let's after him,

---

34 **Wanton in fulness**: are unrestrained.   **43 And bind . . .
you**: and put me further in your debt.   **44 The rest . . . you**:
the rest which is not used in your service is no true repose.   52
the eye wink at: let the eye be blind to what the hand does.
be: be done.

Whose care is gone before to bid us welcome:
It is a peerless kinsman.   [*Flourish. Exeunt.*

Scene V. INVERNESS. MACBETH'S CASTLE

Enter LADY MACBETH, *reading a letter.*

*They met me in the day of success; and I have learned
by the perfectest report, they have more in them than
mortal knowledge. When I burned in desire to question
them further, they made themselves air, into which they
vanished. Whiles I stood rapt in the wonder of it, came* 5
*missives from the king, who all-hailed me, 'Thane of
Cawdor;' by which title, before, these weird sisters saluted
me, and referred me to the coming on of time, with, 'Hail,
king that shalt be!' This have I thought good to deliver
thee, my dearest partner of greatness, that thou mightest* 10
*not lose the dues of rejoicing, by being ignorant of what
greatness is promised thee. Lay it to thy heart, and farewell.*

Glamis thou art, and Cawdor; and shalt be
What thou art promis'd. Yet do I fear thy nature;   15
It is too full o' the milk of human kindness
To catch the nearest way; thou wouldst be great,
Art not without ambition, but without
The illness should attend it; what thou wouldst highly,
That thou wouldst holily; wouldst not play false,   20
And yet wouldst wrongly win; thou'dst have, great
     Glamis,
That which cries, 'Thus thou must do, if thou have it;'

58 **peerless:** unrivalled, without equal.   6 **missives:** messen-
gers.   8 **the coming on of time:** the future.   11 **dues
of rejoicing:** the share of rejoicing due to her. (She is to be his
'partner of greatness'.)   19 **The illness. . . it:** the evil qualities
which should accompany it [*N*].   21 **have** must be understood in
two different senses. Lady Macbeth says (1) thou wouldst **have** the
sovereignty (l. 21); (2) thou wouldst **have** the deed done (ll. 23-4).

And that which rather thou dost fear to do
Than wishest should be undone. Hie thee hither,
That I may pour my spirits in thine ear,   25
And chastise with the valour of my tongue
All that impedes thee from the golden round,
Which fate and metaphysical aid doth seem
To have thee crown'd withal.

Enter a Messenger.

What is your tidings?

Messenger. The king comes here to-night.
Lady Macbeth.   Thou'rt mad to say it.
Is not thy master with him? who, were't so,   31
Would have inform'd for preparation.
    Messenger. So please you, it is true: our thane is coming;
One of my fellows had the speed of him,
Who, almost dead for breath, had scarcely more   35
Than would make up his message.
    Lady Macbeth.   Give him tending;
He brings great news.—[*Exit* Messenger.] The raven him-
        self is hoarse
That croaks the fatal entrance of Duncan
Under my battlements. Come, you spirits
That tend on mortal thoughts! unsex me here,   40
And fill me from the crown to the toe top full
Of direst cruelty; make thick my blood,
Stop up the access and passage to remorse,
That no compunctious visitings of nature

27 **golden round:** the crown.   28 **metaphysical:** supernatural.   29 **withal:** with.   32 **Would . . . preparation:**
would have sent word, bidding us prepare.   34 **had . . . him:**
outrode him.   38 **entrance:** scan *ent(e)rance* (three syllables).
40 **mortal:** deadly.   **unsex me:** take away my womanliness.
42–3 **make thick . . . remorse:** make my feelings numb and in-
accessible to pity.   43 **access:** scan **accéss.**   44 **no . . . nature:**
no natural feelings of compunction.

Shake my fell purpose, nor keep peace between   45
The effect and it! Come to my woman's breasts,
And take my milk for gall, you murdering ministers,
Wherever in your sightless substances
You wait on nature's mischief! Come, thick night,
And pall thee in the dunnest smoke of hell,   50
That my keen knife see not the wound it makes,
Nor heaven peep through the blanket of the dark,
To cry, 'Hold, hold!'

Enter MACBETH.

                  Great Glamis! worthy Cawdor!
Greater than both, by the all-hail hereafter!
Thy letters have transported me beyond   55
This ignorant present, and I feel now
The future in the instant.
  Macbeth.   My dearest love,
Duncan comes here to-night.
  Lady Macbeth.   And when goes hence?
  Macbeth. To-morrow, as he purposes.
  Lady Macbeth.   O! never
Shall sun that morrow see.   60
Your face, my thane, is as a book where men
May read strange matters. To beguile the time,
Look like the time; bear welcome in your eye,

45–6 nor keep . . . it: nor intrude between my purpose and the
achievement of it. ('keep peace': use the restraining power of a
peacemaker.)   **47 for gall:** i.e. as gall *or* in exchange for [N].
murdering ministers: spirits or impulses which prompt to murder.
48 sightless substances: invisible forms.   **49 wait . . . mischief:** aid the destructive forces in nature.   **50 pall:** wrap.
dunnest: darkest.   **52 the blanket . . . dark:** the thick covering
of darkness.   **54 all-hail hereafter:** promise of kingship in
the future [N].   **57 in the instant:** in the present moment.
62–3 To beguile . . . time: suit your looks to the present occasion
in order to be the master of it.

Your hand, your tongue: look like the innocent flower,
But be the serpent under 't. He that's coming   65
Must be provided for; and you shall put
This night's great business into my dispatch;
Which shall to all our nights and days to come
Give solely sovereign sway and masterdom.
   Macbeth. We will speak further.
   Lady Macbeth.   Only look up clear; 70
To alter favour ever is to fear.
Leave all the rest to me.   [*Exeunt.*

Scene VI. THE SAME. BEFORE THE CASTLE

Hautboys and torches. Enter DUNCAN, MALCOLM,
DONALBAIN, BANQUO, LENNOX, MACDUFF, ROSS, ANGUS,
and Attendants.

   Duncan. This castle hath a pleasant seat; the air
Nimbly and sweetly recommends itself
Unto our gentle senses.
   Banquo.   This guest of summer,
The temple-haunting martlet, does approve
By his lov'd mansionry that the heaven's breath   5
Smells wooingly here: no jutty, frieze,
Buttress, nor coign of vantage, but this bird
Hath made his pendent bed and procreant cradle:
Where they most breed and haunt, I have observ'd
The air is delicate.

---

  67 dispatch: management.   **69 solely:** for us alone.   **70–1**
Only . . . fear: keep your looks unembarrassed: to change countenance is always to betray signs of fear. (**Favour** = face, expression.)
4 martlet: i.e. house-martin [*N*].   **approve:** give proof, attest.
5 By . . . mansionry: by making it his favourite abode [*N*].   **6**
jutty: projection.   **7 coign of vantage:** convenient corner.
8 pendent bed: hanging nest.   **procreant cradle:** cradle for
begetting offspring.

Enter LADY MACBETH.

Duncan.   See, see, our honour'd hostess!   10
The love that follows us sometime is our trouble,
Which still we thank as love. Herein I teach you
How you shall bid God 'eyld us for your pains,
And thank us for your trouble.

Lady Macbeth.   All our service,
In every point twice done, and then done double,   15
Were poor and single business, to contend
Against those honours deep and broad wherewith
Your majesty loads our house: for those of old,
And the late dignities heap'd up to them,
We rest your hermits.

Duncan.   Where's the Thane of Cawdor?   20
We cours'd him at the heels, and had a purpose
To be his purveyor; but he rides well,
And his great love, sharp as his spur, hath holp him
To his home before us. Fair and noble hostess,
We are your guest to-night.

Lady Macbeth.   Your servants ever   25
Have theirs, themselves, and what is theirs, in compt,
To make their audit at your highness' pleasure,
Still to return your own.

Duncan.   Give me your hand;
Conduct me to mine host: we love him highly,
And shall continue our graces towards him.   30
By your leave, hostess.   [*Exeunt.*

11 **sometime:** at times.   **is our trouble:** gives us trouble [*N*].
13 **bid God 'eyld us:** pray God reward us, i.e. show us signs of
gratitude [*N*].   16 **single:** slight (cf. I. iii. 140).   19 **heap'd**
. . . them: bestowed in addition to them.   20 **hermits:** beads-
men, whose duty it was to pray for benefactors.   21 **cours'd:**
pursued.   22 **purveyor:** one who went in advance to provide food.
23 **holp:** helped.   26 **theirs:** i.e. their servants.   **what is**
theirs: all their resources.   **in compt:** ready to be accounted
for (as if they were Duncan's property).   28 **Still:** always.

Scene VII. The Same. A Room in the Castle

Hautboys and torches. Enter, and pass over the stage, a Sewer, *and divers* Servants *with dishes and service. Then, enter* MACBETH.

Macbeth. If it were done when 'tis done, then 'twere well
It were done quickly; if the assassination
Could trammel up the consequence, and catch
With his surcease success; that but this blow
Might be the be-all and the end-all here,   5
But here, upon this bank and shoal of time,
We'd jump the life to come. But in these cases
We still have judgment here; that we but teach
Bloody instructions, which, being taught, return
To plague the inventor; this even-handed justice   10
Commends the ingredients of our poison'd chalice
To our own lips. He's here in double trust:
First, as I am his kinsman and his subject,
Strong both against the deed; then, as his host,
Who should against his murderer shut the door,   15
Not bear the knife myself. Besides, this Duncan
Hath borne his faculties so meek, hath been
So clear in his great office, that his virtues
Will plead like angels trumpet-tongu'd against
The deep damnation of his taking-off;   20
And pity, like a naked new-born babe,
Striding the blast, or heaven's cherubin, hors'd

(*s.d.*) *Sewer*: the chief waiter.   **1 If . . . done**: if the act could be
wholly finished when once the blow has been struck. (The sense depends on the two possible meanings of the word 'done') [*N*].   **3
trammel up**: entangle, prevent.   **3-4 catch . . . success**:
obtain success with its cessation (i.e. the cessation of the consequence;
his = its).   **4 that.** See note, I. ii. 60.   **6 But here**: only
here [*N*].   **7 jump**: hazard.   **17 borne . . . meek**: used his
powers so modestly.   **18 clear**: irreproachable.

Upon the sightless couriers of the air,
Shall blow the horrid deed in every eye,
That tears shall drown the wind. I have no spur   25
To prick the sides of my intent, but only
Vaulting ambition, which o'er-leaps itself
And falls on the other.—

Enter LADY MACBETH.

                 How now! what news?
    Lady Macbeth. He has almost supp'd: why have you left
      the chamber?
    Macbeth. Hath he ask'd for me?
    Lady Macbeth.   Know you not he has?   30
    Macbeth. We will proceed no further in this business:
He hath honour'd me of late; and I have bought
Golden opinions from all sorts of people,
Which would be worn now in their newest gloss,
Not cast aside so soon.
    Lady Macbeth.   Was the hope drunk,   35
Wherein you dress'd yourself? hath it slept since,
And wakes it now, to look so green and pale
At what it did so freely? From this time
Such I account thy love. Art thou afeard
To be the same in thine own act and valour   40
As thou art in desire? Wouldst thou have that
Which thou esteem'st the ornament of life,
And live a coward in thine own esteem,
Letting 'I dare not' wait upon 'I would,'

---

   23 sightless: invisible.   **couriers of the air**: winds.   **25–7**
I have . . . ambition: I have nothing but ambition to spur me on
(i.e. no grievance against Duncan) [*N*].   **27 o'er-leaps itself**: over-
reaches itself [*N*].   **28 the other** (side).   **34 would be worn**: need
to be worn.   **37 green**: as after intoxication.   **pale**: with
fear.   **39 Such**: i.e. as valueless, because as fickle as your own
resolution.   **42 ornament of life**: the 'golden opinions' of l. 33.
44 Letting . . . would: Letting fears attend ambition.

Like the poor cat i' the adage?

    Macbeth.   Prithee, peace.   45

I dare do all that may become a man;

Who dares do more is none.

    Lady Macbeth.   What beast was 't, then,

That made you break this enterprise to me?

When you durst do it, then you were a man;

And, to be more than what you were, you would   50

Be so much more the man. Nor time nor place

Did then adhere, and yet you would make both:

They have made themselves, and that their fitness now

Does unmake you. I have given suck, and know

How tender 'tis to love the babe that milks me: 55

I would, while it was smiling in my face,

Have pluck'd my nipple from his boneless gums,

And dash'd the brains out, had I so sworn as you

Have done to this.

    Macbeth.   If we should fail,—

    Lady Macbeth.   We fail?

But screw your courage to the sticking-place,   60

And we'll not fail. When Duncan is asleep,

Whereto the rather shall his day's hard journey

Soundly invite him, his two chamberlains

Will I with wine and wassail so convince,

That memory, the warder of the brain,   65

Shall be a fume, and the receipt of reason

A limbeck only; when in swinish sleep

---

45 **adage:** proverb [*N*].   47 **none:** no man, i.e. something
inferior to a man.   48 **break:** disclose.   50 **to be more
. . . were:** i.e. by actually performing it.   52 **adhere:** fit (the
deed).   60 **But:** only.   **screw . . . place:** screw up your
courage firmly.   64 **wassail:** carousing.   **convince:** overcome.
65-7 **That memory . . . only.** Memory, which forms the outworks
of the brain, is to be confused (by the fumes of intoxication), and
the brain itself (the receipt, or receptacle, of reason) shall become an
'alembic' or vessel for distilling.

Their drenched natures lie, as in a death,
What cannot you and I perform upon
The unguarded Duncan? what not put upon　　　　70
His spongy officers, who shall bear the guilt
Of our great quell?

    Macbeth.　　　　　　Bring forth men-children only;
For thy undaunted mettle should compose
Nothing but males. Will it not be receiv'd,
When we have mark'd with blood those sleepy two　　75
Of his own chamber and us'd their very daggers,
That they have done 't?

    Lady Macbeth.　　　　Who dares receive it other,
As we shall make our griefs and clamour roar
Upon his death?

    Macbeth.　　　I am settled, and bend up
Each corporal agent to this terrible feat.　　　　80
Away, and mock the time with fairest show:
False face must hide what the false heart doth know.

                           [Exeunt.

---

  71 spongy: absorbing drink.　　　**72 quell:** murder.　　　**77 other:** otherwise.　　　**78 As:** seeing that.　　　**79 bend up:** as of a bow prepared for shooting.　　　**80 corporal agent:** bodily faculty.

ACT II

Scene I. INVERNESS. COURT WITHIN THE CASTLE

Enter BANQUO *and* FLEANCE, *with a* Servant *bearing
a torch before him.*

Banquo. How goes the night, boy?
Fleance. The moon is down; I have not heard the clock.
Banquo. And she goes down at twelve.
Fleance.   I take 't, 'tis later, sir.
Banquo. Hold, take my sword. There's husbandry in
   heaven;
Their candles are all out. Take thee that too.   5
A heavy summons lies like lead upon me,
And yet I would not sleep: merciful powers!
Restrain in me the cursed thoughts that nature
Gives way to in repose.

Enter MACBETH, *and a Servant with a torch.*

                              Give me my sword.—
Who's there?   10
Macbeth. A friend.
Banquo. What, sir! not yet at rest? The king's a-bed:
He hath been in unusual pleasure, and
Sent forth great largess to your offices.
This diamond he greets your wife withal,   15
By the name of most kind hostess; and shut up
In measureless content.

---

4 husbandry: thrift.   **5 Take . . . too.** Banquo has handed
Fleance his sword; he now gives him some piece of his armour.
6 heavy summons: (i.e. to sleep).   **14 largess:** gift of money.
offices: servants' quarters.   **15 withal:** with.   **16 by the
name of:** calling her (at the same time).   **shut up:** i.e. ended
the day.

Macbeth.   Being unprepar'd,
Our will became the servant to defect,
Which else should free have wrought.

Banquo.   All's well.
I dreamt last night of the three weird sisters: 20
To you they have show'd some truth.

Macbeth.   I think not of them:
Yet, when we can entreat an hour to serve,
We would spend it in some words upon that business,
If you would grant the time.

Banquo.   At your kind'st leisure.

Macbeth. If you shall cleave to my consent, when 'tis,
It shall make honour for you.

Banquo.   So I lose none   26
In seeking to augment it, but still keep
My bosom franchis'd and allegiance clear,
I shall be counsell'd.

Macbeth.   Good repose the while!

Banquo. Thanks, sir: the like to you.   30

                  [*Exeunt* BANQUO *and* FLEANCE.

Macbeth. Go bid thy mistress, when my drink is ready
She strike upon the bell. Get thee to bed.

                        [*Exit* Servant.

Is this a dagger which I see before me,
The handle toward my hand? Come, let me clutch thee:
I have thee not, and yet I see thee still.   35
Art thou not, fatal vision, sensible
To feeling as to sight? or art thou but
A dagger of the mind, a false creation,

18–19 **Our will . . . wrought:** i.e. Macbeth's will did not have
free play in the entertainment of Duncan.   22 **when . . . serve:**
when I can command an hour of your time to be at my service.
(Macbeth uses the royal 'we' as if he were already king.)   25 **If
you . . . 'tis:** if you will co-operate with me when the time is ripe
[*N*].   26 **So:** provided that.   28 **franchis'd: free** (from guilt).
36 **sensible:** palpable to the senses. Cf. l. 40.

Proceeding from the heat-oppressed brain?
I see thee yet, in form as palpable   40
As this which now I draw.
Thou marshall'st me the way that I was going;
And such an instrument I was to use.
Mine eyes are made the fools o' the other senses,
Or else worth all the rest: I see thee still;   45
And on thy blade and dudgeon gouts of blood,
Which was not so before. There's no such thing:
It is the bloody business which informs
Thus to mine eyes. Now o'er the one half-world
Nature seems dead, and wicked dreams abuse   50
The curtain'd sleep; witchcraft celebrates
Pale Hecate's offerings; and wither'd murder,
Alarum'd by his sentinel, the wolf,
Whose howl's his watch, thus with his stealthy pace,
With Tarquin's ravishing strides, toward his design   55
Moves like a ghost. Thou sure and firm-set earth,
Hear not my steps, which way they walk, for fear
Thy very stones prate of my whereabout,
And take the present horror from the time,
Which now suits with it. Whiles I threat, he lives: 60
Words to the heat of deeds too cold breath gives.

                                        [*A bell rings.*

I go, and it is done; the bell invites me.
Hear it not, Duncan; for it is a knell
That summons thee to heaven or to hell.

---

40 **yet**: still.   **44–5 Mine eyes ... rest**: either my eyes are
the dupes of the other senses (which persuade me that the dagger
is real), or else they are truer witnesses than the rest of them.
46 **dudgeon**: hilt.   **gouts**: drops.   **48–9 informs Thus to**:
takes this form before.   **50 abuse**: deceive.   **52 Pale
Hecate's offerings**: offerings to pale Hecate [*N*].   **54 watch**:
sentinel-cry.   59–60 **take ... suits with it**: break the silence
which suits the moment so well.

Scene II. The Same

Enter LADY MACBETH.

Lady Macbeth. That which hath made them drunk hath
    made me bold,
What hath quench'd them hath given me fire. Hark!
Peace!
It was the owl that shriek'd, the fatal bellman,
Which gives the stern'st good-night. He is about it: 5
The doors are open, and the surfeited grooms
Do mock their charge with snores: I have d ugg'd their
    possets,
That death and nature do contend about them,
Whether they live or die.
    Macbeth. [*Within.*] Who's there? what, ho!   10
    Lady Macbeth. Alack! I am afraid they have awak'd.
And 'tis not done; the attempt and not the deed
Confounds us. Hark! I laid their daggers ready;
He could not miss them. Had he not resembled
My father as he slept, I had done 't. My husband!   15

Enter MACBETH.

Macbeth. I have done the deed. Didst thou not hear a
    noise?
Lady M. I heard the owl scream and the crickets cry.
Did not you speak?
    Macbeth.   When?
    Lady Macbeth.   Now.
    Macbeth.   As I descended?
    Lady Macbeth. Ay.
    Macbeth. Hark!   20

2 **given me fire:** inflamed my courage.   5 **He:** Macbeth.
8 **possets.** A posset was a hot drink taken about bedtime.   12–13
the attempt . . . confounds us: to attempt the deed and fail is fatal
to us.

Who lies i' the second chamber?

  Lady Macbeth.   Donalbain.

  Macbeth. [*Looking on his hands.*] This is a sorry sight.

  Lady Macbeth. A foolish thought to say a sorry sight.

  Macbeth. There's one did laugh in 's sleep, and one cried
    'Murder!'

That they did wake each other: I stood and heard them;

But they did say their prayers, and address'd them   26

Again to sleep.

  Lady Macbeth. There are two lodg'd together.

  Macbeth. One cried 'God bless us!' and 'Amen' the other:

As they had seen me with these hangman's hands.

Listening their fear, I could not say 'Amen,'   30

When they did say 'God bless us!'

  Lady Macbeth.   Consider it not so deeply.

  Macbeth. But wherefore could not I pronounce 'Amen'?

I had most need of blessing, and 'Amen'

Stuck in my throat.

  Lady Macbeth.   These deeds must not be thought

After these ways; so, it will make us mad.   35

  Macbeth. Methought I heard a voice cry 'Sleep no more!

Macbeth does murder sleep,' the innocent sleep,

Sleep that knits up the ravell'd sleave of care,

The death of each day's life, sore labour's bath,

Balm of hurt minds, great nature's second course,   40

Chief nourisher in life's feast,—

  Lady Macbeth.   What do you mean?

  Macbeth. Still it cried, 'Sleep no more!' to all the house:

'Glamis hath murder'd sleep, and therefore Cawdor

Shall sleep no more, Macbeth shall sleep no more!'

---

  26 address'd them: prepared themselves.   **29 As:** as
if [*N*].   **38 knits up . . . care:** smoothes out, or puts
in order, the tangled skein of care [*N*].   **40 second course.**
Sleep is the second course at the banquet of life, the first being
labour.

Lady Macbeth. Who was it that thus cried ? Why, worthy
 thane,   45
You do unbend your noble strength to think
So brainsickly of things. Go get some water,
And wash this filthy witness from your hand.
Why did you bring these daggers from the place ?
They must lie there : go carry them, and smear 50
The sleepy grooms with blood.
 Macbeth.   I'll go no more :
I am afraid to think what I have done ;
Look on 't again I dare not.
 Lady Macbeth.   Infirm of purpose !
Give me the daggers. The sleeping and the dead
Are but as pictures ; 'tis the eye of childhood 55
That fears a painted devil. If he do bleed,
I'll gild the faces of the grooms withal ;
For it must seem their guilt.

        [*Exit. Knocking within.*
 Macbeth.   Whence is that knocking ?
How is 't with me, when every noise appals me ?
What hands are here ! Ha ! they pluck out mine eyes. 60
Will all great Neptune's ocean wash this blood
Clean from my hand ? No, this my hand will rather
The multitudinous seas incarnadine,
Making the green one red.

     Re-enter LADY MACBETH.

Lady M. My hands are of your colour, but I shame 65
To wear a heart so white.—[*Knocking within.*] I hear a
 knocking
At the south entry ; retire we to our chamber ;

---

 46 **unbend :** cf. I. vii. 79, 'bend up'. **48 filthy witness :**
stains which provide evidence against you. **56 painted devil :**
picture of the devil [*N*]. **63 incarnadine :** make the colour of
crimson.

A little water clears us of this deed;
How easy is it, then! Your constancy
Hath left you unattended. [*Knocking within.*] Hark!
    more knocking.   70
Get on your night-gown, lest occasion call us,
And show us to be watchers. Be not lost
So poorly in your thoughts.
    Macbeth. To know my deed 'twere best not know myself.
                             [*Knocking within.*
Wake Duncan with thy knocking! I would thou couldst!
                                       [*Exeunt.*

Scene III. THE SAME

Knocking within. Enter a Porter.

    Porter. Here's a knocking, indeed! If a man were
porter of hell-gate, he should have old turning the key.
[*Knocking within.*] Knock, knock, knock! Who's
there, i' the name of Beelzebub? Here's a farmer that
hanged himself on the expectation of plenty: come in   5
time; have napkins enough about you; here you'll
sweat for 't. [*Knocking within.*] Knock, knock! Who's
there, i' the other devil's name! Faith, here's an equivocator, that could swear in both the scales against either
scale; who committed treason enough for God's sake,   10
yet could not equivocate to heaven: O! come in, equivocator. [*Knocking within.*] Knock, knock, knock! Who's
there? Faith, here's an English tailor come hither for

69–70 **Your constancy . . . unattended:** your firmness has deserted you.   71 **night-gown:** dressing-gown. Cf. v. i. 5.   72
watchers: i.e. awake.   73 **poorly:** miserably.   74 **To know my
deed . . . know myself:** if I must look my deed in the face, it would
be better to lose consciousness.   2 **old:** plenty of (archaic).   6
napkins: handkerchiefs.   8 **the other devil's name.** He now
alludes to Satan, having already sworn by Beelzebub.   8–9
equivocator: one who uses religious terms in order to deceive others
[*N*].   9 **the scales:** i.e. of justice.

stealing out of a French hose: come in, tailor; here you
may roast your goose. [*Knocking within.*] Knock,   15
knock; never at quiet! What are you? But this place
is too cold for hell. I'll devil-porter it no further: I had
thought to have let in some of all professions, that go
the primrose way to the everlasting bonfire. [*Knocking
within.*] Anon, anon! I pray you, remember the porter.   20
                                    [*Opens the gate.*

Enter MACDUFF *and* LENNOX.

Macduff. Was it so late, friend, ere you went to bed,
That you do lie so late?
  Porter. Faith, sir, we were carousing till the second cock.
  Macduff. Is thy master stirring?

Enter MACBETH.

Our knocking has awak'd him; here he comes.   25
  Lennox. Good morrow, noble sir.
  Macbeth.   Good morrow, both.
  Macduff. Is the king stirring, worthy thane?
  Macbeth.   Not yet.
  Macduff. He did command me to call timely on him:
I have almost slipp'd the hour.
  Macbeth.   I'll bring you to him.
  Macduff. 1 know this is a joyful trouble to you;   30
But yet 'tis one.
  Macbeth. The labour we delight in physics pain.
This is the door.
  Macduff.   I'll make so bold to call,
For 'tis my limited service.   [*Exit.*
  Lennox. Goes the king hence to-day?
  Macbeth.   He does: he did appoint so.
  Lennox. The night has been unruly: where we lay,   36

15 **goose**: a tailor's smoothing iron.   20 **anon**: cf. 1. i. 10.
23 **second cock**: about 3 a.m. [*N*].   32 **physics**: is remedy for.
34 **limited**: appointed.

Our chimneys were blown down; and, as they say,
Lamentings heard i' the air; strange screams of death,
And prophesying with accents terrible
Of dire combustion and confus'd events   40
New hatch'd to the woeful time. The obscure bird
Clamour'd the livelong night: some say the earth
Was feverous and did shake.
   Macbeth.   'Twas a rough night.
   Lennox. My young remembrance cannot parallel
A fellow to it.   45

Re-enter MACDUFF.

   Macduff. O horror! horror! horror! Tongue nor heart
Cannot conceive nor name thee!
   Macbeth. |
   Lennox. | What's the matter?
   Macduff. Confusion now hath made his masterpiece!
Most sacrilegious murder hath broke ope
The Lord's anointed temple, and stole thence   50
The life o' the building!
   Macbeth. What is 't you say? the life?
   Lennox. Mean you his majesty?
   Macduff. Approach the chamber, and destroy your sight
With a new Gorgon: do not bid me speak;   55
See, and then speak yourselves.
             [*Exeunt* MACBETH *and* LENNOX.
                 Awake! awake!
Ring the alarum-bell. Murder and treason!
Banquo and Donalbain! Malcolm! awake!

---

   40 combustion: not literally 'burning', but metaphorically 'confusion'.   **41 New hatch'd:** newly born. The unlucky time is
saddled with an evil offspring.   **The obscure bird:** bird of
darkness, the owl (accent óbscure).   **48 Confusion:** destruction.
55 Gorgon: In Greek mythology there were three Gorgons, one of
whom, Medusa, turned the beholder to stone.

Shake off this downy sleep, death's counterfeit,
And look on death itself! up, up, and see　　　　　　60
The great doom's image! Malcolm! Banquo!
As from your graves rise up, and walk like sprites,
To countenance this horror! Ring the bell.　　　[*Bell rings.*

Enter LADY MACBETH.

Lady Macbeth. What's the business,
That such a hideous trumpet calls to parley　　　　65
The sleepers of the house? speak, speak!
　　Macduff.　　　　　　　　　　　O gentle lady!
'Tis not for you to hear what I can speak;
The repetition in a woman's ear
Would murder as it fell.

Enter BANQUO.

　　　　　　　　　　　O Banquo! Banquo!
Our royal master's murder'd!
　　Lady Macbeth.　　　　　　Woe, alas!　　　　70
What! in our house?
　　Banquo.　　　　　　Too cruel any where.
Dear Duff, I prithee, contradict thyself,
And say it is not so.

Re-enter MACBETH *and* LENNOX.

Macbeth. Had I but died an hour before this chance
I had liv'd a blessed time; for, from this instant,　　75
There's nothing serious in mortality,
All is but toys; renown and grace is dead,
The wine of life is drawn, and the mere lees
Is left this vault to brag of.

59 **death's counterfeit:** the image or picture of death.　　61
The great doom's image: a picture of the Day of Judgement.
62 **sprites:** spirits, ghosts.　　　63 **To countenance:** to be in
accord with [*N*].　　76 **mortality:** human life.　　79 **this vault:**
the world which is 'vaulted' by the sky.

Enter MALCOLM *and* DONALBAIN.

Donalbain. What is amiss?

Macbeth.   You are, and do not know 't:
The spring, the head, the fountain of your blood   81
Is stopp'd; the very source of it is stopp'd.

Macduff. Your royal father's murder'd.

Malcolm.   O! by whom?

Lennox. Those of his chamber, as it seem'd, had done 't:
Their hands and faces were all badg'd with blood;   85
So were their daggers, which unwip'd we found
Upon their pillows: they star'd, and were distracted; no
    man's life
Was to be trusted with them.

Macbeth. O! yet I do repent me of my fury,
That I did kill them.

Macduff.   Wherefore did you so?   90

Macb. Who can be wise, amaz'd, temperate and furious,
Loyal and neutral, in a moment? No man:
The expedition of my violent love
Outran the pauser, reason. Here lay Duncan,
His silver skin lac'd with his golden blood;   95
And his gash'd stabs look'd like a breach in nature
For ruin's wasteful entrance: there, the murderers,
Steep'd in the colours of their trade, their daggers
Unmannerly breech'd with gore: who could refrain,
That had a heart to love, and in that heart   100
Courage to make 's love known?

Lady Macbeth.   Help me hence, ho!

85 **badg'd:** marked (as with a tradesman's badge).   91
amaz'd. The word had a stronger sense in Shakespeare's time, almost
that of 'demented'.   93 **expedition:** speed.   94 **pauser:**
one who stops or hesitates.   95 **His silver . . . blood:** his
white skin was like a garment of silver 'laced' or diversified with
streaks of 'golden' blood [N].   97 **ruin's:** destruction's.
99 **Unmannerly . . . gore:** clothed with gore after their rude (unmannerly) assault on Duncan.   101 **make 's:** make his.

Macduff. Look to the lady.

Malcolm. [*Aside to* DONALBAIN.] Why do we hold our
    tongues,
That most may claim this argument for ours?

Donalbain. [*Aside to* MALCOLM.] What should be spoken
Here where our fate, hid in an auger-hole,   · 106
May rush and seize us? Let's away: our tears
Are not yet brew'd.

Malcolm. [*Aside to* DONALBAIN.] Nor our strong sorrow
Upon the foot of motion.

Banquo.   Look to the lady: 110
                    [LADY MACBETH *is carried out.*

And when we have our naked frailties hid,
That suffer in exposure, let us meet,
And question this most bloody piece of work,
To know it further. Fears and scruples shake us:
In the great hand of God I stand, and thence   115
Against the undivulg'd pretence I fight
Of treasonous malice.

Macduff.   And so do I.

All.   So all.

Macbeth. Let's briefly put on manly readiness,
And meet i' the hall together.

All.   ·   Well contented.

                    [*Exeunt all but* MALCOLM *and* DONALBAIN.

Mal. What will you do? Let's not consort with them:
To show an unfelt sorrow is an office   121

---

104 **argument:** theme.   106 **auger-hole:** minute hole [*N*].
108 **brew'd:** i.e. fully mature.   109–10 **Nor . . . motion:** i.e.
our feelings of sorrow are paralysed by their own strength.   ('upon
the foot of motion': ready for action.)   111–12 **when . . .
exposure:** when we have covered our half-dressed bodies which are
likely to suffer from exposure.   113 **question:** examine.   114
scruples: doubts.   116 **undivulg'd pretence:** the design as yet
unrevealed.   118 **manly readiness:** warlike equipment and
temper. Cf. ll. 111–12.   121 **office:** function, duty.

Which the false man does easy. I'll to England.

   Donalbain. To Ireland, I; our separated fortune
Shall keep us both the safer: where we are,
There's daggers in men's smiles: the near in blood,   125
The nearer bloody.

   Malcolm.   This murderous shaft that's shot
Hath not yet lighted, and our safest way
Is to avoid the aim: therefore, to horse;
And let us not be dainty of leave-taking,
But shift away: there's warrant in that theft   130
Which steals itself when there's no mercy left. [*Exeunt*

Scene IV. THE SAME. WITHOUT THE CASTLE

Enter ROSS *and an* OLD MAN.

   Old Man. Threescore and ten I can remember well;
Within the volume of which time I have seen
Hours dreadful and things strange, but this sore night
Hath trifled former knowings.

   Ross.   Ah! good father,
Thou seest, the heavens, as troubled with man's act,   5
Threaten his bloody stage: by the clock 'tis day,
And yet dark night strangles the travelling lamp.
Is 't night's predominance, or the day's shame,
That darkness does the face of earth entomb,
When living light should kiss it?

   Old Man.   'Tis unnatural,   10
Even like the deed that 's done. On Tuesday last,

125-6 **the near . . . bloody:** the nearer his kinship to us, the
nearer our danger [*N*].   130-1 **there's warrant . . . left:**
there is good authority for the theft of stealing ourselves away,
seeing that there is no hope of mercy.   4 **Hath . . . knowings:**
has dwarfed my past experience.   6 **bloody stage:** i.e. the earth.
7 **travelling lamp:** the sun.   8 **Is 't night's . . . shame:** does
the evil influence of the night (of the murder) extend to the present
time, or is the day ashamed to witness (what the night has done)?

A falcon, towering in her pride of place,
Was by a mousing owl hawk'd at and kill'd.

  Ross. And Duncan's horses,—a thing most strange and
    certain,—

Beauteous and swift, the minions of their race,   15
Turn'd wild in nature, broke their stalls, flung out,
Contending 'gainst obedience, as they would
Make war with mankind.

  Old Man.   'Tis said they eat each other.

  Ross. They did so, to the amazement of mine eyes,
That look'd upon 't. Here comes the good Macduff.   20

Enter MACDUFF.

How goes the world, sir, now?

  Macduff.   Why, see you not?

  Ross. Is 't known who did this more than bloody deed?

  Macduff. Those that Macbeth hath slain.

  Ross.   Alas, the day!
What good could they pretend?

  Macduff.   They were suborn'd.

Malcolm and Donalbain, the king's two sons,   25
Are stol'n away and fled, which puts upon them
Suspicion of the deed.

  Ross.   'Gainst nature still!
Thriftless ambition, that wilt ravin up
Thine own life's means! Then 'tis most like
The sovereignty will fall upon Macbeth.   30

  Macduff. He is already nam'd, and gone to Scone
To be invested.

  Ross.   Where is Duncan's body?

12 **place:** the point or pitch attained by a falcon . . . before stooping
down on its quarry (*O.E.D.*).   13 **mousing:** (usually) mouse-
catching.   15 **minions:** cf. I. ii. 19.   24 **good:** advantage.
pretend: intend, design.   27 **still:** always. Cf. III. i. 22.
28 **ravin up:** devour.   29 **Thine . . . means:** the source of
thine own existence.

Macduff. Carried to Colmekill,
The sacred storehouse of his predecessors
And guardian of their bones.

Ross.   Will you to Scone?   35

Macduff. No, cousin, I'll to Fife.

Ross.   Well, I will thither.

Macduff. Well, may you see things well done there: adieu!
Lest our old robes sit easier than our new!

Ross. Farewell, father.

Old Man. God's benison go with you; and with those 40
That would make good of bad, and friends of foes!

                               [*Exeunt.*

38 **Lest . . . new:** lest our new robes should sit less easily on us
than our old, i.e. lest the new reign make us regret the old.   40
benison: blessing.   41 **of:** out of.

ACT III

Scene I. FORRES. A ROOM IN THE PALACE

Enter BANQUO.

Banquo. Thou hast it now: King, Cawdor, Glamis, all,
As the weird women promis'd; and, I fear,
Thou play'dst most foully for 't; yet it was said
It should not stand in thy posterity,
But that myself should be the root and father   5
Of many kings. If there come truth from them,—
As upon thee, Macbeth, their speeches shine,—
Why, by the verities on thee made good,
May they not be my oracles as well,
And set me up in hope? But, hush! no more.   10

> *Sennet sounded. Enter* MACBETH, *as king*; LADY MAC-
> BETH, *as queen*; LENNOX, ROSS, Lords, Ladies, *and*
> Attendants.

Macbeth. Here's our chief guest.
Lady Macbeth.   If he had been forgotten,
It had been as a gap in our great feast,
And all-thing unbecoming.
Macbeth. To-night we hold a solemn supper, sir,
And I'll request your presence.
Banquo.   Let your highness   15
Command upon me; to the which my duties
Are with a most indissoluble tie
For ever knit.
Macbeth. Ride you this afternoon?

---

7 shine: appear with all the lustre of conspicuous truth (Johnson).   **8 verities:** actualities [*N*].   (*s.d.*) *Sennet:* a set of notes
on the trumpet or cornet.   **13 all-thing:** wholly, altogether [*N*].
16 the which (i.e. your commands).

Banquo. Ay, my good lord. 20

Macbeth. We should have else desir'd your good advice—
Which still hath been both grave and prosperous—
In this day's council; but we'll take to-morrow.
Is 't far you ride?

Banquo. As far, my lord, as will fill up the time 25
'Twixt this and supper; go not my horse the better,
I must become a borrower of the night
For a dark hour or twain.

Macbeth.   Fail not our feast.

Banquo. My lord, I will not.

Macbeth. We hear our bloody cousins are bestow'd 30
In England and in Ireland, not confessing
Their cruel parricide, filling their hearers
With strange invention; but of that to-morrow,
When therewithal we shall have cause of state
Craving us jointly. Hie you to horse; adieu 35
Till you return at night. Goes Fleance with you?

Banquo. Ay, my good lord: our time does call upon 's.

Macbeth. I wish your horses swift and sure of foot;
And so I do commend you to their backs.
Farewell.   [*Exit* BANQUO.
Let every man be master of his time 41
Till seven at night; to make society
The sweeter welcome, we will keep ourself
Till supper-time alone; while then, God be with you!
                [*Exeunt all but* MACBETH *and an Attendant.*
Sirrah, a word with you. Attend those men 45

22 **still**: always. Cf. II. iv. 27.   26 **this**: this time.   **go not**
. . . **better**: if my horse go (subjunctive) not the better; i.e. so
much the more quickly in view of the distance to be covered.
30 **are bestow'd**: have settled.   32 **parricide**: here, the murder
of their father. (The word is more often used of the criminal.)   34–5
cause . . . jointly: state affairs requiring our joint attention.
37 **our time . . . upon 's**: we must be off.   43 **the sweeter**
welcome: more to be welcomed.   44 **while**: till.

Our pleasure?

   Attendant. They are, my lord, without the palace gate.

   Macbeth. Bring them before us. [*Exit* Attendant.] To
     be thus is nothing;

But to be safely thus. Our fears in Banquo

Stick deep, and in his royalty of nature   50

Reigns that which would be fear'd: 'tis much he dares,

And, to that dauntless temper of his mind,

He hath a wisdom that doth guide his valour

To act in safety. There is none but he

Whose being I do fear; and under him   55

My genius is rebuk'd, as it is said

Mark Antony's was by Caesar. He chid the sisters

When first they put the name of king upon me,

And bade them speak to him; then, prophet-like,

They hail'd him father to a line of kings.   60

Upon my head they plac'd a fruitless crown,

And put a barren sceptre in my gripe,

Thence to be wrench'd with an unlineal hand,

No son of mine succeeding. If 't be so,

For Banquo's issue have I fil'd my mind;   65

For them the gracious Duncan have I murder'd;

Put rancours in the vessel of my peace

Only for them; and mine eternal jewel

Given to the common enemy of man,

To make them kings, the seed of Banquo kings!   70

Rather than so, come fate into the list,

And champion me to the utterance! Who's there?

---

    49 But to be safely thus (i.e. enthroned). The sentence requires
some such conclusion as 'is everything'.   **51 would be fear'd:** needs
to be feared.   **52 to:** in addition to.   **56 genius:** tutelary spirit
[*N*].   **63 with:** by. **unlineal:** not of my line [*N*].   **65 fil'd:**
defiled.   **68 mine eternal jewel:** my immortal soul.   **69 the
common . . . man:** the enemy of the whole race, i.e. the Devil.   **71–2**
Macbeth challenges fate to enter the lists and fight (champion) him
to the death.   **72 to the utterance:** to the uttermost (*à outrance*).

Re-enter Attendant, *with two* Murderers.

Now go to the door, and stay there till we call.   •

              [*Exit* Attendant.

Was it not yesterday we spoke together?

  First Murderer. It was, so please your highness.

  Macbeth.   Well then, now

Have you consider'd of my speeches? Know   76

That it was he in the times past which held you

So under fortune, which you thought had been

Our innocent self. This I made good to you

In our last conference, pass'd in probation with you,   80

How you were borne in hand, how cross'd, the instruments,

Who wrought with them, and all things else that might

To half a soul and to a notion craz'd

Say, 'Thus did Banquo.'

  First Murderer.   You made it known to us.

  Macbeth. I did so; and went further, which is now   85

Our point of second meeting. Do you find

Your patience so predominant in your nature

That you can let this go? Are you so gospell'd

To pray for this good man and for his issue,

Whose heavy hand hath bow'd you to the grave   90

And beggar'd yours for ever?

  First Murderer.   We are men, my liege.

  Macbeth. Ay, in the catalogue ye go for men;

As hounds and greyhounds, mongrels, spaniels, curs,

Shoughs, water-rugs, and demi-wolves, are clept

---

79 **made good:** showed, proved.   80 **pass'd . . . you:** went over the proofs with you.   81 **borne in hand:** deluded, abused with false hopes.   **cross'd:** thwarted.   **the instruments:** the means employed.   83 **to a notion craz'd:** even to a fool. (Notion = understanding.)   86 **Our point of:** the reason for our.   88 **so gospell'd:** so well instructed in the Gospel as to. (See St. Matthew v. 44: 'pray for them which despitefully use you').   91 **yours:** your issue.   94 **Shoughs:** a kind of lap-dog.   **water-rugs:** shaggy water-dogs.   **demi-wolves:** cross-breeds.   **clept:** called.

All by the name of dogs: the valu'd file   95
Distinguishes the swift, the slow, the subtle,
The housekeeper, the hunter, every one
According to the gift which bounteous nature
Hath in him clos'd; whereby he does receive
Particular addition, from the bill   100
That writes them all alike: and so of men.
Now, if you have a station in the file,
Not i' the worst rank of manhood, say it;
And I will put that business in your bosoms,
Whose execution takes your enemy off,   105
Grapples you to the heart and love of us,
Who wear our health but sickly in his life,
Which in his death were perfect.

  Second Murderer.   I am one, my liege,
Whom the vile blows and buffets of the world
Have so incens'd that I am reckless what   110
I do to spite the world.

  First Murderer.   And I another,
So weary with disasters, tugg'd with fortune,
That I would set my life on any chance,
To mend it or be rid on 't.

  Macbeth.   Both of you
Know Banquo was your enemy.

  Second Murderer.   True, my lord.   115
  Macbeth. So is he mine; and in such bloody distance

---

95 **the valu'd file**: the graded list.   97 **The housekeeper:**
the watch-dog.   99 **clos'd:** enclosed.   99–100: **whereby . . . bill**: whereby he receives a special title, distinguishing him
from the list, &c.   102–3 **Now . . . say it.** The Murderers must prove by their compliance that their place in the
list of mankind is above the lowest.   105 **Whose execution:** the performance of which.   **takes . . . off.** See I.
vii. 20 [*N*].   107 **in his life:** while he lives.   112 **tugg'd:**
pulled this way and that.   **with:** by (as often).   116 **in . . .
distance:** in such bloody alienation [*N*].

That every minute of his being thrusts
Against my near'st of life: and though I could
With bare-fac'd power sweep him from my sight
And bid my will avouch it, yet I must not,   120
For certain friends that are both his and mine,
Whose loves I may not drop, but wail his fall
Whom I myself struck down; and thence it is
That I to your assistance do make love,
Masking the business from the common eye   125
For sundry weighty reasons.
  Second Murderer.   We shall, my lord,
Perform what you command us.
  First Murderer.   Though our lives—
  Macbeth. Your spirits shine through you. Within this
      hour at most
I will advise you where to plant yourselves,
Acquaint you with the perfect spy o' the time,   130
The moment on 't; for 't must be done to-night,
And something from the palace; always thought
That I require a clearness: and with him—
To leave no rubs nor botches in the work—
Fleance his son, that keeps him company,   135
Whose absence is no less material to me
Than is his father's, must embrace the fate
Of that dark hour. Resolve yourselves apart;
I'll come to you anon.

117–18 **every minute . . . life:** i.e. every minute he lives is a
stab to the principle of my life ('my near'st of life': that on which
my life depends). 119 **bare-fac'd:** unmasked.   120 **And bid . . .
it:** and make my mere will its justification.   121 **For:** because of.
122 **but wail his fall:** i.e. must bewail his fall.   130 **the perfect
. . . time:** the fit moment as determined by the closest scrutiny [*N*].
132 **something from:** at some distance from.   132–3 **always
. . . clearness:** it being always remembered that my reputation
must remain unsullied.   134 **rubs:** roughnesses, a metaphor from
bowls (a 'rub' is an obstacle or impediment by which a bowl is
diverted from its proper course).

Second Murderer. We are resolv'd, my lord.

Macbeth. I'll call upon you straight: abide within.

[*Exeunt* Murderers.

It is concluded: Banquo, thy soul's flight,　141
If it find heaven, must find it out to-night.　[*Exit.*

Scene II. THE SAME. ANOTHER ROOM IN THE PALACE

Enter LADY MACBETH *and a* Servant.

Lady Macbeth. Is Banquo gone from court?

Servant. Ay, madam, but returns again to-night.

Lady Macbeth. Say to the king, I would attend his leisure
For a few words.

Servant.　Madam, I will.　[*Exit.*

Lady Macbeth.　Nought's had, all's spent,
Where our desire is got without content:　5
'Tis safer to be that which we destroy
Than by destruction dwell in doubtful joy.

Enter MACBETH.

How now, my lord! why do you keep alone,
Of sorriest fancies your companions making,
Using those thoughts which should indeed have died　10
With them they think on? Things without all remedy
Should be without regard: what's done is done.

Macbeth. We have scotch'd the snake, not kill'd it:
She'll close and be herself, whilst our poor malice
Remains in danger of her former tooth.　15
But let the frame of things disjoint, both the worlds suffer,
Ere we will eat our meal in fear, and sleep
In the affliction of these terrible dreams
That shake us nightly. Better be with the dead,

7 **by destruction:** by destroying some one else.　13 **scotch'd:**
cut, gashed [*N*].　15 **former tooth:** the tooth she had before the
'scotching', and still has.　16 **the frame of things:** the universe.
disjoint: fall asunder. **both the worlds:** heaven and earth.

Whom we, to gain our peace, have sent to peace,   20
Than on the torture of the mind to lie
In restless ecstasy. Duncan is in his grave;
After life's fitful fever he sleeps well;
Treason has done his worst: nor steel, nor poison,
Malice domestic, foreign levy, nothing   25
Can touch him further.

   Lady Macbeth.   Come on;
Gentle my lord, sleek o'er your rugged looks;
Be bright and jovial among your guests to-night.

   Macbeth. So shall I, love; and so, I pray, be you.
Let your remembrance apply to Banquo;   30
Present him eminence, both with eye and tongue:
Unsafe the while, that we
Must lave our honours in these flattering streams,
And make our faces vizards to our hearts,
Disguising what they are.

   Lady Macbeth.   You must leave this.   35

   Macbeth. O! full of scorpions is my mind, dear wife;
Thou know'st that Banquo and his Fleance lives.

   Lady Macbeth. But in them nature's copy's not eterne.

   Macbeth. There's comfort yet; they are assailable;
Then be thou jocund. Ere the bat hath flown   40
His cloister'd flight, ere to black Hecate's summons
The shard-born beetle with his drowsy hums
Hath rung night's yawning peal, there shall be done
A deed of dreadful note.

   Lady Macbeth.   What's to be done?

   22 ecstasy: the state of being 'beside oneself' [N].   **24 his:**
its.   **27 sleek o'er:** smooth down (like hair).   **30 apply
to:** be given to.   **31 Present him eminence:** pay him special
honour.   **32 Unsafe:** it *or* we being unsafe [N].   **34
vizards:** masks.   **38 copy:** copyhold or lease. Nature has not
given them an eternal lease of life.   **41 cloister'd:** among
cloisters.   **42 shard-born:** born in dung [N].   **43
yawning peal:** the peal which invites to slumber.

Macbeth. Be innocent of the knowledge, dearest chuck,
Till thou applaud the deed. Come, seeling night,   **46**
Scarf up the tender eye of pitiful day,
And with thy bloody and invisible hand
Cancel and tear to pieces that great bond
Which keeps me pale! Light thickens, and the crow   **50**
Makes wing to the rooky wood;
Good things of day begin to droop and drowse,
Whiles night's black agents to their preys do rouse.
Thou marvell'st at my words: but hold thee still;
Things bad begun make strong themselves by ill: **55**
So, prithee, go with me.   [*Exeunt.*

Scene III. THE SAME. A PARK, WITH A ROAD
LEADING TO THE PALACE

Enter three Murderers.

First Murderer. But who did bid thee join with us?
Third Murderer.   Macbeth.
Sec. Mur. He needs not our mistrust, since he delivers
Our offices and what we have to do
To the direction just.
First Murderer.   Then stand with us.
The west yet glimmers with some streaks of day: **5**
Now spurs the lated traveller apace
To gain the timely inn; and near approaches
The subject of our watch.
Third Murderer.   Hark! I hear horses.
Banquo. [Within.] Give us a light there, ho!
Second Murderer.   Then 'tis he: the rest
That are within the note of expectation   **10**

---

46 **seeling:** blinding [*N*].   49 **bond:** the bond by which Banquo
and Fleance hold their lives from Nature [*N*].   2–4 **He needs
. . . just:** he (the third Murderer) need not be distrusted by us, since
his account of what we have to do is in exact agreement with our
instructions.   6 **lated:** belated.   10 **note of expectation:** the
list of those expected at supper.

Already are i' the court.

First Murderer.   His horses go about.

Third Murderer. Almost a mile; but he does usually,
So all men do, from hence to the palace gate
Make it their walk.

Second Murderer. A light, a light!

Third Murderer.   'Tis he.

First Murderer. Stand to 't.   15

    Enter BANQUO *and* FLEANCE, *with a torch.*

Banquo. It will be rain to-night.

First Murderer.   Let it come down.

                            [*They set upon* BANQUO.

Banquo. O, treachery! Fly, good Fleance, fly, fly, fly!
Thou mayst revenge. O slave!

                            [*Dies.* FLEANCE *escapes.*

Third Murderer. Who did strike out the light?

First Murderer.   Was 't not the way?

Third Murderer. There's but one down; the son is fled.

Second Murderer.   We have lost 20
Best half of our affair.

First Murderer. Well, let's away, and say how much is
    done.   [*Exeunt.*

Scene IV. THE SAME. A ROOM OF STATE IN THE
                    PALACE

A Banquet prepared. Enter MACBETH, LADY MACBETH,
    ROSS, LENNOX, Lords, *and* Attendants.

Macbeth. You know your own degrees; sit down: at first
    and last,
The hearty welcome.

---

   11 **go about:** take the long horse-path to the castle.   **16 Let**
. . . down: let a storm of blows descend on his head.   **19 the**
way: the best way, the thing to do.   **1 degrees:** ranks.   **at first**
and last: once and for all.   **2 The:** i.e. the welcome proper to
the occasion.

✗*Lords.*   Thanks to your majesty.

Macbeth. Ourself will mingle with society
And play the humble host.
Our hostess keeps her state, but in best time   5
We will require her welcome.

Lady Macbeth. Pronounce it for me, sir, to all our friends;
For my heart speaks they are welcome.

Enter First Murderer, *to the door.*

Macb. See, they encounter thee with their hearts' thanks;
Both sides are even: here I'll sit i' the midst: 10
Be large in mirth; anon, we'll drink a measure
The table round. [*Approaching the door.*] There's blood
          upon thy face.

✗ *Murderer.* 'Tis Banquo's, then.

Macbeth. 'Tis better thee without than he within.
Is he dispatch'd?   15

✗ *Murderer.* My lord, his throat is cut; that I did for him.

Macbeth. Thou art the best o' the cut-throats; yet he's
          good
That did the like for Fleance: if thou didst it,
Thou art the nonpareil.

✗ *Murderer.*   Most royal sir,
Fleance is 'scap'd.   20

Macb. Then comes my fit again: I had else been perfect;
Whole as the marble, founded as the rock,
As broad and general as the casing air:
But now I am cabin'd, cribb'd, confined, bound in

3 **society**: the company.   5 **state**: a raised chair, with a
canopy, &c.; a throne (*O.E.D.*).   6 **require her welcome**: ask
her to welcome you.   11 **large**: free, generous.   14 **'Tis
. . . within**: it is better that the blood should be outside you than
inside him [*N*].   19 **nonpareil**: one without equal.   21 **fit**: i.e.
of terror.   22 **Whole as the marble**: sound as solid marble.
founded: immovable, steady.   23 **general**: free, unfettered.
casing: enclosing, surrounding.

To saucy doubts and fears. But Banquo's safe? 25

✗*Murderer*. Ay, my good lord; safe in a ditch he bides,
With twenty trenched gashes on his head,
The least a death to nature.

Macbeth. Thanks for that.
There the grown serpent lies: the worm that 's fled
Hath nature that in time will venom breed, 30
No teeth for the present. Get thee gone; to-morrow
We'll hear ourselves again. [*Exit* Murderer.

Lady Macbeth, My royal lord,
You do not give the cheer: the feast is sold
That is not often vouch'd, while 'tis a-making,
'Tis given with welcome: to feed were best at home; 35
From thence, the sauce to meat is ceremony;
Meeting were bare without it.

Macbeth. Sweet remembrancer!
Now good digestion wait on appetite,
And health on both!

Lennox. May it please your highness sit?
[*The Ghost of* BANQUO *enters, and
sits in* MACBETH'S *place.*

Macbeth. Here had we now our country's honour roof'd,
Were the grac'd person of our Banquo present; 41
Who may I rather challenge for unkindness
Than pity for mischance!

✗*Ross*. His absence, sir,
Lays blame upon his promise. Please 't your highness ⟶

---

25 **saucy**: insolent (a stronger word than now). 27 **trenched**:
cut (Fr. *trancher*). 28 **a death to nature**: enough to kill a
man. 29 **worm**: a small serpent. 32 **We'll . . . again**: we
will speak together again [*N*]. 33 **cheer**: friendly encouragement [*N*]. 36 **From thence**: away from home. **ceremony**: three syllables, cer(e)mony. 40 **Here . . . present**:
if Banquo were here, all that is most honourable in the country would
be assembled under one roof. 42 **may I rather challenge**: I
hope I may rather reprove.

To grace us with your royal company.   45

Macbeth. The table's full.

Lennox.   Here is a place reserv'd, sir.

Macbeth. Where?

Lennox. Here, my good lord. What is 't that moves your
highness?

Macbeth. Which of you have done this?

Lords.   What, my good lord?

Macbeth. Thou canst not say I did it: never shake   50
Thy gory locks at me.

Ross. Gentlemen, rise; his highness is not well.

Lady Macbeth. Sit, worthy friends: my lord is often thus,
And hath been from his youth: pray you, keep seat;
The fit is momentary; upon a thought   55
He will again be well. If much you note him,
You shall offend him and extend his passion:
Feed, and regard him not. Are you a man?

Macbeth. Ay, and a bold one, that dare look on that
Which might appal the devil.

Lady Macbeth.   O proper stuff!   60
This is the very painting of your fear;
This is the air-drawn dagger which, you said,
Led you to Duncan. O! these flaws and starts—
Impostors to true fear—would well become
A woman's story at a winter's fire,   65
Authoriz'd by her grandam. Shame itself!
Why do you make such faces? When all 's done,
You look but on a stool.

Macbeth. Prithee, see there! behold! look! lo! how say you?
Why, what care I? If thou canst nod, speak too.   70

---

55 **upon a thought:** with the speed of thought.   57 **extend
his passion:** prolong the attack.   60 **proper:** used ironically,
cf. 'fine'.   62 **air-drawn:** imaginary.   63 **flaws:** sudden
gusts (of passion).   64 **to:** compared to.   66 **Authoriz'd:**
vouched for.   **Shame itself:** you are the very picture of shame.

If charnel-houses and our graves must send
Those that we bury back, our monuments
Shall be the maws of kites.   [*Ghost disappears.*
  Lady Macbeth.   What! quite unmann'd in folly?
  Macbeth. If I stand here, I saw him.
  Lady Macbeth.   Fie, for shame!
  Macbeth. Blood hath been shed ere now, i' the olden
    time,   75
Ere human statute purg'd the gentle weal;
Ay, and since too, murders have been perform'd
Too terrible for the ear: the times have been,
That, when the brains were out, the man would die,
And there an end; but now they rise again,   80
With twenty mortal murders on their crowns,
And push us from our stools: this is more strange
Than such a murder is.
  Lady Macbeth.   My worthy lord,
Your noble friends do lack you.
  Macbeth.   I do forget.
Do not muse at me, my most worthy friends;   85
I have a strange infirmity, which is nothing
To those that know me. Come, love and health to all;
Then, I'll sit down. Give me some wine; fill full.
I drink to the general joy of the whole table,
And to our dear friend Banquo, whom we miss;   90
Would he were here! to all, and him, we thirst,
And all to all.
  ✗*Lords.*   Our duties, and the pledge.

---

71 **charnel-house:** house or vault in which dead bodies are piled.
72 **monuments:** tombs [*N*].   73 **maw** = stomach.   76
human: humane.   **gentle weal:** purged the commonwealth
(weal) and made it gentle, or civilized.   81 **mortal murders:**
fatal wounds. Cf. III. iv. 27–8.   85 **muse:** be in amazement.
92 **all to all:** (I thirst to pledge) all good wishes to all the company.
Our duties . . . pledge: we offer our allegiance and return the
wishes.

Re-enter Ghost

Macbeth. Avaunt! and quit my sight! Let the earth hide
thee!
Thy bones are marrowless, thy blood is cold;
Thou hast no speculation in those eyes   95
Which thou dost glare with.

Lady Macbeth.   Think of this, good peers,
But as a thing of custom: 'tis no other;
Only it spoils the pleasure of the time.

Macbeth. What man dare, I dare:
Approach thou like the rugged Russian bear,   100
The arm'd rhinoceros, or the Hyrcan tiger;
Take any shape but that, and my firm nerves
Shall never tremble: or be alive again,
And dare me to the desart with thy sword;
If trembling I inhabit then, protest me   105
The baby of a girl. Hence, horrible shadow!
Unreal mockery, hence!   [*Ghost vanishes.*
                    Why, so; being gone,
I am a man again. Pray you, sit still.

Lady Macbeth. You have displac'd the mirth, broke the
good meeting,
With most admir'd disorder.

Macbeth.   Can such things be   110
And overcome us like a summer's cloud,
Without our special wonder? You make me strange
Even to the disposition that I owe,

95 **speculation:** intelligent or comprehending vision.   97 **a
thing of custom:** a habit of his. Cf. ll. 53–4.   101 **arm'd:** i.e.
with hide and horn [*N*].   104 **to the desart:** to solitary combat
(desart = desert).   105 **If trembling I inhabit:** if I remain
trembling [*N*].   106 **The baby of a girl:** a girl's doll.   107
being gone: now that it is gone (loose grammar).   110 **admir'd:**
causing wonder.   111 **overcome us:** pass over us.   112–13 **You
make . . . owe:** you make me a stranger to my natural disposition, so
that I am not myself (owe = own).

When now I think you can behold such sights,
And keep the natural ruby of your cheeks,   115
When mine are blanch'd with fear.

   Ross.   What sights, my lord?

   Lady Macbeth. I pray you, speak not; he grows worse and
     worse;
Question enrages him. At once, good-night:
Stand not upon the order of your going,
But go at once.

   Lennox.   Good-night; and better health   120
Attend his majesty!

   Lady Macbeth.   A kind good-night to all!

                          [*Exeunt* Lords *and* Attendants.

   Macbeth. It will have blood, they say; blood will have
     blood:
Stones have been known to move and trees to speak;
Augurs and understood relations have
By maggot-pies and choughs and rooks brought forth
The secret'st man of blood. What is the night?   126

   Lady Macbeth. Almost at odds with morning, which is
     which.

   Macbeth. How sayst thou, that Macduff denies his person
At our great bidding?

   Lady Macbeth.   Did you send to him, sir?

   Macbeth. I hear it by the way; but I will send.   130
There's not a one of them but in his house
I keep a servant fee'd. I will to-morrow—
And betimes I will—to the weird sisters:
More shall they speak; for now I am bent to know,

---

  119 **Stand . . . going:** do not insist on precedence.   124
Augurs: auguries or prognostication by omens [*N*].   125
maggot-pies: magpies; **choughs:** jackdaws.   126 **What . . .
night?** What time of night is it?   127 **at odds:** at issue.
128–9 **How sayst . . . bidding?** What do you say as to Macduff's
refusal to attend at my bidding?

By the worst means, the worst. For mine own good   **135**
All causes shall give way: I am in blood
Stepp'd in so far, that, should I wade no more,
Returning were as tedious as go o'er.
Strange things I have in head that will to hand,
Which must be acted ere they may be scann'd.   **140**
    Lady Macbeth. You lack the season of all natures, sleep.
    Macbeth. Come, we'll to sleep. My strange and self-abuse
Is the initiate fear that wants hard use:
We are yet but young in deed.   *[Exeunt.*

Scene V. A Heath

Thunder. Enter the three Witches, *meeting* HECATE.

    First Witch. Why, how now, Hecate! you look angerly.
    Hecate. Have I not reason, beldams as you are,
Saucy and overbold? How did you dare
To trade and traffic with Macbeth
In riddles and affairs of death;   **5**
And I, the mistress of your charms,
The close contriver of all harms,
Was never call'd to bear my part,
Or show the glory of our art?
And, which is worse, all you have done   **10**
Hath been but for a wayward son,
Spiteful and wrathful; who, as others do,
Loves for his own ends, not for you.
But make amends now: get you gone,

---

138 **Returning . . . o'er:** it would be as tedious to return as to
go over to the opposite side.   139–40 **Strange . . . scann'd:**
I have projects which I intend to execute first and to examine after.
141 **season:** that which 'seasons' or brings into a healthy condition.
142–3 **My strange . . . use:** my strange self-deception is the beginner's fear that is not yet hardened by custom.   1 **angerly:**
in an angry way.   2 **beldams:** old hags.   7 **close contriver:**
secret plotter.

And at the pit of Acheron 15
Meet me i' the morning: thither he
Will come to know his destiny:
Your vessels and your spells provide,
Your charms and every thing beside.
I am for the air; this night I'll spend 20
Unto a dismal and a fatal end:
Great business must be wrought ere noon:
Upon the corner of the moon
There hangs a vaporous drop profound;
I'll catch it ere it come to ground: 25
And that distill'd by magic sleights
Shall raise such artificial sprites
As by the strength of their illusion
Shall draw him on to his confusion:
He shall spurn fate, scorn death, and bear 30
His hopes 'bove wisdom, grace, and fear;
And you all know, security
Is mortals' chiefest enemy.

            [*Song within*, 'Come away, come away,' &c.
Hark! I am call'd; my little spirit, see, 34
Sits in a foggy cloud, and stays for me.   [*Exit.*
First Witch. Come, let's make haste; she'll soon be back
  again.   [*Exeunt.*

Scene VI. Forres. A Room in the Palace

Enter lennox *and another* lord.

Lennox. My former speeches have but hit your thoughts,
Which can interpret further: only, I say,

15 **pit of Acheron:** i.e. the witches' cavern of iv. i [*N*].　21 **unto:**
working for.　24 **profound:** either 'deep, and therefore ready to
fall' or 'having deep or mysterious qualities'.　26 **sleights:** arts,
devices.　27 **artificial sprites:** the 'Apparitions' of Act iv, Sc. i
(sprites = spirits).　28 **their illusion:** their power of deceiving.　29
confusion: destruction.　32 **security:** careless confidence (*not* safety,
but the feeling of it).　1 i.e. 'I have been hinting at more than I said.'

Things have been strangely borne. The gracious Duncan
Was pitied of Macbeth: marry, he was dead:
And the right-valiant Banquo walk'd too late;   5
Whom, you may say, if 't please you, Fleance kill'd,
For Fleance fled: men must not walk too late.
Who cannot want the thought how monstrous
It was for Malcolm and for Donalbain
To kill their gracious father? damned fact!   10
How it did grieve Macbeth! did he not straight
In pious rage the two delinquents tear,
That were the slaves of drink and thralls of sleep?
Was not that nobly done? Ay, and wisely too;
For 'twould have anger'd any heart alive   15
To hear the men deny 't. So that, I say,
He has borne all things well; and I do think
That, had he Duncan's sons under his key,—
As, an 't please heaven, he shall not,—they should find
What 'twere to kill a father; so should Fleance.   20
But, peace! for from broad words, and 'cause he fail'd
His presence at the tyrant's feast, I hear
Macduff lives in disgrace. Sir, can you tell
Where he bestows himself?
    Lord.   The son of Duncan,
From whom this tyrant holds the due of birth,   25
Lives in the English court, and is receiv'd
Of the most pious Edward with such grace
That the malevolence of fortune nothing
Takes from his high respect. Thither Macduff
Is gone to pray the holy king, upon his aid   30

    3 borne: managed (so in l. 17).   **4 marry:** indeed! here = 'well
then!'   **8 Who . . . thought?** who *can* help thinking? (want =
be without, lack) [N].   **10 fact:** deed.   **19 an:** if.   **21
broad words:** plain speaking.   **21–2 fail'd His presence:**
failed to present himself.   **25 holds:** withholds.   **29
his high respect:** the respect in which he is held.   **30 upon his
aid:** in his aid (i.e. of Duncan's son, Malcolm).

To wake Northumberland and war-like Siward:
That, by the help of these—with him above
To ratify the work—we may again
Give to our tables meat, sleep to our nights,
Free from our feasts and banquets bloody knives,   35
Do faithful homage and receive free honours;
All which we pine for now. And this report
Hath so exasperate the king that he
Prepares for some attempt of war.

   Lennox.   Sent he to Macduff?

   Lord. He did: and with an absolute, 'Sir, not I,'   40
The cloudy messenger turns me his back,
And hums, as who should say, 'You'll rue the time
That clogs me with this answer.'

   Lennox.   And that well might
Advise him to a caution to hold what distance
His wisdom can provide. Some holy angel   45
Fly to the court of England and unfold
His message ere he come, that a swift blessing
May soon return to this our suffering country
Under a hand accurs'd!

   Lord.   I'll send my prayers with him!

                                          [Exeunt.

---

35 **Free**: remove [*N*].   36 **free**: i.e. from servility on our part or flattery on the king's.   38 **exasperate**: exasperated.   **40–3 with an absolute . . . this answer**: on receiving a flat refusal, the sullen messenger turned his back, and muttered as one who would say: 'You will regret the time when you burdened me with so disagreeable a message' [*N*].   **44–5 hold . . . provide**: keep as far away as he can.

ACT IV

Scene I. A Cavern. In the middle, a boiling Cauldron

Thunder. Enter the three Witches.

First Witch.	Thrice the brinded cat hath mew'd.
Second Witch.	Thrice and once the hedge-pig whin'd.
Third Witch.	Harper cries: 'Tis time, 'tis time.
First Witch.	Round about the cauldron go;
	In the poison'd entrails throw. 5
	Toad, that under cold stone
	Days and nights hast thirty-one
	Swelter'd venom sleeping got,
	Boil thou first i' the charmed pot.
All.	Double, double toil and trouble; 10
	Fire burn and cauldron bubble.
Second Witch.	Fillet of a fenny snake,
	In the cauldron boil and bake;
	Eye of newt, and toe of frog,
	Wool of bat, and tongue of dog, 15
	Adder's fork, and blind-worm's sting,
	Lizard's leg, and howlet's wing,
	For a charm of powerful trouble,
	Like a hell-broth boil and bubble.
All.	Double, double toil and trouble; 20
	Fire burn and cauldron bubble.
Third Witch.	Scale of dragon, tooth of wolf,
	Witches' mummy, maw and gulf

1 **brinded**: brindled, streaked.   2 **hedge-pig**: hedgehog.
3 **Harper**: either the name of an unknown demon, or a variation of
'harpy', a mythical rapacious monster [N].   8 **Swelter'd**:
sweated out. **got**: produced, begotten.   12 **fillet**: slice. **fenny**:
living in fens.   16 **fork**, i.e. forked tongue. **blind-worm**:
slow-worm [N].   17 **howlet**: owl.   23 **mummy**: a medical
preparation of the substance of mummies.   **maw**: cf. III. iv. 73.
gulf: i.e. greedy stomach [N].

Of the ravin'd salt-sea shark,
Root of hemlock digg'd i' the dark, 25
Liver of blaspheming Jew,
Gall of goat, and slips of yew
Sliver'd in the moon's eclipse,
Nose of Turk, and Tartar's lips,
Finger of birth-strangled babe 30
Ditch-deliver'd by a drab,
Make the gruel thick and slab:
Add thereto a tiger's chaudron,
For the ingredients of our cauldron.

All.   Double, double toil and trouble; 35
Fire burn and cauldron bubble.

Second Witch. Cool it with a baboon's blood,
Then the charm is firm and good.

Enter HECATE.

Hecate.   O! well done! I commend your pains,
And every one shall share i' the gains. 40
And now about the cauldron sing,
Like elves and fairies in a ring,
Enchanting all that you put in.
        [*Music and a song,* 'Black Spirits,' &c.

Second Witch. By the pricking of my thumbs,
Something wicked this way comes. 45
        Open, locks,
        Whoever knocks.

Enter MACBETH.

Macbeth. How now, you secret, black, and midnight hags!
What is 't you do?

All.   A deed without a name.

---

24 **ravin'd**: ravenous.   28 **sliver'd**: slit off.   31 **Ditch-deliver'd**: born in a ditch.   **drab**: prostitute.   32 **slab**: slushy.   33 **chaudron**: entrails.   37 **baboon**: accent báboon.

Macbeth. I conjure you, by that which you profess,— 50
Howe'er you come to know it,—answer me:
Though you untie the winds and let them fight
Against the churches; though the yesty waves
Confound and swallow navigation up;
Though bladed corn be lodg'd and trees blown down; 55
Though castles topple on their warders' heads;
Though palaces and pyramids do slope
Their heads to their foundations; though the treasure
Of Nature's germens tumble all together,
Even till destruction sicken; answer me 60
To what I ask you.
  First Witch.   Speak.
  Second Witch.   Demand.
  Third Witch.   We'll answer.
  First Witch. Say if thou'dst rather hear it from our
    mouths,
Or from our masters'?
  Macbeth.   Call 'em: let me see 'em.
  First Witch. Pour in sow's blood, that hath eaten
        Her nine farrow; grease that's sweaten 65
        From the murderer's gibbet throw
        Into the flame.
  All.   Come, high or low;
        Thyself and office deftly show.

    Thunder. First Apparition *of an armed Head.*

  Macbeth. Tell me, thou unknown power,—
  First Witch.   He knows thy thought:
Hear his speech, but say thou nought. 70

50 **profess:** claim to have knowledge of.   53 **yesty:** yeasty,
frothy.   54 **navigation:** ships.   55 **bladed:** in the blade.
lodg'd: laid, flattened.   59 **germens:** germs, seeds.   65 **Her
nine farrow:** her litter of nine.   68 **office:** function; supply
'thy' from 'thyself'.

First Apparition. Macbeth! Macbeth! Macbeth! beware
 Macduff;
Beware the Thane of Fife. Dismiss me. Enough.
                                        [*Descends.*
Macbeth. Whate'er thou art, for thy good caution thanks;
Thou hast harp'd my fear aright. But one word more,—
First Witch. He will not be commanded: here's another,
More potent than the first.   76

Thunder. Second Apparition, *a bloody Child.*

Second Apparition. Macbeth! Macbeth! Macbeth!—
Macbeth. Had I three ears, I'd hear thee.
Second Apparition. Be bloody, bold, and resolute; laugh
 to scorn
The power of man, for none of woman born   80
Shall harm Macbeth.   [*Descends.*
Macbeth. Then live, Macduff: what need I fear of thee?
But yet I'll make assurance double sure,
And take a bond of fate: thou shalt not live;
That I may tell pale-hearted fear it lies,   85
And sleep in spite of thunder.

Thunder. Third Apparition, *a Child crowned, with
 a tree in his hand.*

                          What is this,
That rises like the issue of a king,
And wears upon his baby brow the round
And top of sovereignty?
    All.   Listen, but speak not to 't.
Third Apparition. Be lion-mettled, proud, and take no care

73 **good caution:** timely warning.   74 **harp'd . . . aright:**
touched the chord of my fear.   78 **three:** one for each call;
i.e. I am *all* attention.   83 **double:** doubly.   84 **take a bond
of fate:** lay fate under an obligation to keep her word (legal metaphor).   88 **round.** See I. v. 27.   89 **top:** crown, with something too of a figurative sense: 'highest symbol.'

Who chafes, who frets, or where conspirers are: 91
Macbeth shall never vanquish'd be until
Great Birnam Wood to high Dunsinane Hill
Shall come against him.   [*Descends.*
  Macbeth.   That will never be:
Who can impress the forest, bid the tree   95
Unfix his earth-bound root? Sweet bodements! good!
Rebellion's head, rise never till the wood
Of Birnam rise, and our high-plac'd Macbeth
Shall live the lease of nature, pay his breath
To time and mortal custom. Yet my heart   100
Throbs to know one thing: tell me—if your art
Can tell so much,—shall Banquo's issue ever
Reign in this kingdom?
  All.   Seek to know no more.
  Macbeth. I will be satisfied: deny me this,
And an eternal curse fall on you! Let me know.   105
Why sinks that cauldron? and what noise is this?
                        [*Hautboys.*
  First Witch. Show!
  Second Witch. Show!
  Third Witch. Show!
  All. Show his eyes, and grieve his heart;   110
Come like shadows, so depart.

A show of Eight Kings; the last with a glass in his hand:
BANQUO'S Ghost *following.*

  Macbeth. Thou art too like the spirit of Banquo; down!
Thy crown does sear mine eyeballs: and thy hair,
Thou other gold-bound brow, is like the first:
A third is like the former. Filthy hags!   115

95 **impress:** press into service.   96 **bodements:** prophecies.
99 **lease of nature:** normal length of life. Cf. III. ii. 38.   100
mortal custom: the common lot of men, i.e. natural death.   106
Hautboys: now called 'oboes'.   110 **show:** (the future to)
his eyes.   (*s.d.*) *show:* dumb-show, pageant [N].

Why do you show me this? A fourth! Start, eyes!
What! will the line stretch out to the crack of doom?
Another yet? A seventh! I'll see no more:
And yet the eighth appears, who bears a glass
Which shows me many more; and some I see   120
That two-fold balls and treble sceptres carry.
Horrible sight! Now, I see, 'tis true;
For the blood-bolter'd Banquo smiles upon me,
And points at them for his.   [*Apparitions vanish.*
                        What! is this so?

  First Witch. Ay, sir, all this is so: but why   125
Stands Macbeth thus amazedly?
Come sisters, cheer we up his sprites,
And show the best of our delights.
I'll charm the air to give a sound,
While you perform your antick round,   130
That this great king may kindly say
Our duties did his welcome pay.
               [*Music. The Witches dance, and then
                          vanish with* HECATE.

  Macbeth. Where are they? Gone? Let this pernicious hour
Stand aye accursed in the calendar!
Come in, without there!

Enter LENNOX.

Lennox.   What's your Grace's will?   135
Macbeth. Saw you the weird sisters?
Lennox.   No, my lord.
Macbeth. Came they not by you?
Lennox.   No indeed, my lord.

116 **Start, eyes:** (from your sockets).   117 **crack of doom:**
the thunder-peal of the Judgement-day.   119 **a glass:** probably
not a mirror but a crystal used for foreseeing the future.   123
blood-bolter'd: having his hair clotted or matted with blood.
130 **antick:** quaint, fantastic.   **round:** a round dance.   132
duties: homage.

Macbeth. Infected be the air whereon they ride,
And damn'd all those that trust them! I did hear
The galloping of horse: who was 't came by?   140
  Lennox. 'Tis two or three, my lord, that bring you word
Macduff is fled to England.
  Macbeth.   Fled to England!
  Lennox. Ay, my good lord.
  Macbeth. Time, thou anticipat'st my dread exploits;
The flighty purpose never is o'ertook   145
Unless the deed go with it; from this moment
The very firstlings of my heart shall be
The firstlings of my hand. And even now,
To crown my thoughts with acts, be it thought and done:
The castle of Macduff I will surprise;   150
Seize upon Fife; give to the edge of the sword
His wife, his babes, and all unfortunate souls
That trace him in his line. No boasting like a fool;
This deed I'll do before this purpose cool:
But no more sights! Where are these gentlemen?   155
Come, bring me where they are.   [*Exeunt.*

Scene II. FIFE. MACDUFF'S CASTLE

Enter LADY MACDUFF, *her* Son, *and* ROSS.

Lady Macduff. What had he done to make him fly the land?
  Ross. You must have patience, madam.
  Lady Macduff.   He had none:
His flight was madness: when our actions do not,
Our fears do make us traitors.
  Ross.   You know not
Whether it was his wisdom or his fear.   5
  Lady Macduff. Wisdom! to leave his wife, to leave his
            babes,

144 **anticipat'st:** forestallest.   145 **flighty:** swift.   147–8
The very . . . my hand: what my heart first conceives my hand
shall first execute.   153 **trace:** follow.

His mansion and his titles in a place
From whence himself does fly? He loves us not;
He wants the natural touch; for the poor wren,
The most diminutive of birds, will fight—   10
Her young ones in her nest—against the owl.
All is the fear and nothing is the love;
As little is the wisdom, where the flight
So runs against all reason.

   Ross.   My dearest coz,
I pray you, school yourself: but, for your husband,   15
He is noble, wise, judicious, and best knows
The fits o' the season. I dare not speak much further:
But cruel are the times, when we are traitors
And do not know ourselves, when we hold rumour
From what we fear, yet know not what we fear,   20
But float upon a wild and violent sea
Each way and move. I take my leave of you:
Shall not be long but I'll be here again.
Things at the worst will cease, or else climb upward
To what they were before. My pretty cousin,   25
Blessing upon you!

   Lady Macduff. Father'd he is, and yet he's fatherless.

   Ross. I am so much a fool, should I stay longer,
It would be my disgrace, and your discomfort:
I take my leave at once.   [*Exit.*

   Lady Macduff.   Sirrah, your father's dead: 30

---

7 titles: the things to which he has a title.   **9 wants:** lacks.
natural touch: natural affection.   **12** i.e. his action shows much
more fear for himself than love for us.   **15 for:** as for.   **17 fits:**
crises [*N*].   **18–19 when we ... ourselves:** when we are held to
be traitors (by others) and do not know ourselves for such.   **19–20**
when we ... fear: when we accept reports which have no source
but our fears.   **22 Each ... move:** (with) each plunge and movement (of the sea) [*N*].   **24** Metaphor from Fortune's wheel.   **28–9**
I am so much ... discomfort: if I stayed longer I should weep,
and so bring disgrace to myself and embarrassment to you [*N*].

And what will you do now? How will you live?

Son. As birds do, mother.

Lady Macduff.   What! with worms and flies?

Son. With what I get, I mean; and so do they.

Lady Macduff. Poor bird! thou'dst never fear the net nor lime,

The pit-fall nor the gin.   35

Son. Why should I, mother? Poor birds they are not set for. My father is not dead, for all your saying.

Lady Macduff. Yes, he is dead: how wilt thou do for a father?

Son. Nay, how will you do for a husband?

Lady Macduff. Why, I can buy me twenty at any market.

Son. Then you'll buy 'em to sell again.   41

Lady Macduff. Thou speak'st with all thy wit; and yet, i' faith,

With wit enough for thee.

Son. Was my father a traitor, mother?

Lady Macduff. Ay, that he was.   45

Son. What is a traitor?

Lady Macduff. Why, one that swears and lies.

Son. And be all traitors that do so?

Lady Macduff. Every one that does so is a traitor, and must be hanged.

Son. And must they all be hanged that swear and lie?

Lady Macduff. Every one.   51

Son. Who must hang them?

Lady Macduff. Why, the honest men.

Son. Then the liars and swearers are fools, for there are liars and swearers enow to beat the honest men, and hang up them.   56

Lady Macduff. Now God help thee, poor monkey!

---

32 with: on   **34 lime:** bird-lime.   **35 gin:** trap, snare.
41 i.e. because you won't want to *keep* all.   **55 enow:** originally a plural form of 'enough'.

But how wilt thou do for a father?

Son. If he were dead, you'd weep for him: if you would not, it were a good sign that I should quickly have a new father. 61

Lady Macduff. Poor prattler, how thou talk'st!

Enter a Messenger.

Mess. Bless you, fair dame! I am not to you known,
Though in your state of honour I am perfect.
I doubt some danger does approach you nearly: 65
If you will take a homely man's advice,
Be not found here; hence, with your little ones.
To fright you thus, methinks, I am too savage;
To do worse to you were fell cruelty,
Which is too nigh your person. Heaven preserve you! 70
I dare abide no longer. [*Exit.*

Lady Macduff. Whither should I fly?
I have done no harm. But I remember now
I am in this earthly world, where to do harm
Is often laudable, to do good sometime
Accounted dangerous folly; why then, alas! 75
Do I put up that womanly defence,
To say I have done no harm?

Enter Murderers.

What are these faces?

Murderer. Where is your husband?

Lady Macduff. I hope in no place so unsanctified
Where such as thou mayst find him.

Murderer. He's a traitor. 80

Son. Thou liest, thou shag-hair'd villain.

---

64 **Though . . . perfect:** though I am perfectly acquainted with your rank. 65 **doubt:** incline to think. 69 **To do worse:** not to give you warning. 74 **sometime:** at times. 81 **shag-hair'd:** having shaggy hair.

Murderer.   What, you egg!
Young fry of treachery!   [*Stabbing him.*
Son.   He has killed me, mother:
Run away, I pray you!   [*Dies.*
                        [*Exit* LADY MACDUFF, *crying ' Murder ',
                                    and pursued by the* Murderers.

Scene III. ENGLAND. BEFORE THE KING'S PALACE

Enter MALCOLM *and* MACDUFF.

Malcolm. Let us seek out some desolate shade, and there
Weep our sad bosoms empty.
Macduff.   Let us rather
Hold fast the mortal sword, and like good men
Bestride our down-fall'n birthdom; each new morn
New widows howl, new orphans cry, new sorrows   5
Strike heaven on the face, that it resounds
As if it felt with Scotland and yell'd out
Like syllable of dolour.
Malcolm.   What I believe I'll wail,
What know believe; and what I can redress,
As I shall find the time to friend, I will.   10
What you have spoke, it may be so perchance.
This tyrant, whose sole name blisters our tongues,
Was once thought honest; you have lov'd him well;
He hath not touch'd you yet. I am young; but something
You may deserve of him through me, and wisdom   15

---

82 **Young fry of treachery:** child of a traitor [*N*].   3 **mortal:**
deadly. **good:** honourable.   4 **Bestride:** defend [*N*]. **birthdom:**
inheritance, birthright, i.e. our country.   7–8 **As if . . . dolour:**
as if sympathy with Scotland made it utter a similar cry of pain.
8 When I am convinced such things have happened, I will lament
them.   10 **to friend:** favourable.   12 **sole name:** mere name.
13 **honest:** honourable.   14–15 **something . . . me:** you may
put him somewhat in your debt by injuring me. ('through me':
i.e. by betraying me.)   **and wisdom:** i.e. and it is wisdom.

To offer up a weak, poor, innocent lamb
To appease an angry god.
 Macduff. I am not treacherous.
 Malcolm.   But Macbeth is.
A good and virtuous nature may recoil
In an imperial charge. But I shall crave your pardon; 20
That which you are my thoughts cannot transpose;
Angels are bright still, though the brightest fell;
Though all things foul would wear the brows of grace,
Yet grace must still look so.
 Macduff.   I have lost my hopes.
 Malcolm. Perchance even there where I did find my
  doubts. 25
Why in that rawness left you wife and child—
Those precious motives, those strong knots of love—
Without leave-taking? I pray you,
Let not my jealousies be your dishonours,
But mine own safeties: you may be rightly just, 30
Whatever I shall think.
 Macduff.   Bleed, bleed, poor country!
Great tyranny, lay thou thy basis sure,
For goodness dare not check thee! wear thou thy wrongs;
The title is affeer'd! Fare thee well, lord:
I would not be the villain that thou think'st 35
For the whole space that's in the tyrant's grasp,
And the rich East to boot.

---

16 **a weak ... lamb**: i.e. Malcolm.   19–20 **may recoil ...
charge**: may fall back (from goodness) in executing a royal command.
21 **transpose**: change [N].   2–4 **Though all ... look so**:
though all evil things should assume the appearance of goodness
('grace'), yet goodness must continue to look like itself [N].   26 **in
that rawness**: so prematurely.   27 **motives**: influences, reasons
for action.   29 **jealousies**: suspicions [N].   32 **sure**: with
confidence, security.   33 **goodness ... thee**: i.e. Malcolm won't
oppose you.   **wear ... wrongs**: flaunt thy crimes.   34 **the
title**: of tyrant.   **affeer'd**: confirmed [N].   37 **to boot**: in addition.

Malcolm.   Be not offended:
I speak not as in absolute fear of you.
I think our country sinks beneath the yoke;
It weeps, it bleeds, and each new day a gash   **40**
Is added to her wounds: I think withal
There would be hands uplifted in my right;
And here from gracious England have I offer
Of goodly thousands: but, for all this,
When I shall tread upon the tyrant's head,   **45**
Or wear it on my sword, yet my poor country
Shall have more vices than it had before,
More suffer, and more sundry ways than ever,
By him that shall succeed.
  Macduff.   What should he be?
  Malcolm. It is myself I mean; in whom I know   **50**
All the particulars of vice so grafted,
That, when they shall be open'd, black Macbeth
Will seem as pure as snow, and the poor state
Esteem him as a lamb, being compar'd
With my confineless harms.
  Macduff.   Not in the legions   **55**
Of horrid hell can come a devil more damn'd
In evils to top Macbeth.
  Malcolm.   I grant him bloody,
Luxurious, avaricious, false, deceitful,
Sudden, malicious, smacking of every sin
That has a name; but there's no bottom, none,   **60**
In my voluptuousness: your wives, your daughters,
Your matrons, and your maids, could not fill up
The cistern of my lust, and my desire

---

38 absolute: certain.   **43 England**: the king of England.
47 have more vices: contain, have to endure more vices.   **52**
open'd: i.e. like buds; (cf. 'grafted').   **55 confineless harms**:
unbridled vices.   **58 luxurious**: lustful.   **59 Sudden**: unexpected in attack.

All continent impediments would o'erbear
That did oppose my will; better Macbeth   65
Than such an one to reign.

Macduff.   Boundless intemperance
In nature is a tyranny; it hath been
Th' untimely emptying of the happy throne,
And fall of many kings. But fear not yet
To take upon you what is yours; you may   70
Convey your pleasures in a spacious plenty,
And yet seem cold, the time you may so hoodwink.
We have willing dames enough; there cannot be
That vulture in you, to devour so many
As will to greatness dedicate themselves,   75
Finding it so inclin'd.

Malcolm.   With this there grows
In my most ill-compos'd affection such
A stanchless avarice that, were I king,
I should cut off the nobles for their lands,
Desire his jewels and this other's house;   80
And my more-having would be as a sauce
To make me hunger more, that I should forge
Quarrels unjust against the good and loyal,
Destroying them for wealth.

Macduff.   This avarice
Sticks deeper, grows with more pernicious root   85
Than summer-seeming lust, and it hath been
The sword of our slain kings: yet do not fear;

64 **continent**: restraining.   67 **hath been**: hath caused.
71 **Convey**: secretly indulge in.   72 **the time**: the world.
75-6 **to greatness dedicate . . . inclin'd**: sacrifice their chastity
to please a king.   77 **ill-compos'd affection**: intemperate
disposition.   78 **stanchless**: unquenchable.   80 **his**:
this one's.   86 **summer-seeming**: resembling summer in
its heat and shortness.   86-7 **and it hath . . . kings**:
i.e. avarice has caused the death of those kings who have been
murdered.

Scotland hath foisons to fill up your will,
Of your mere own; all these are portable,
With other graces weigh'd.   90

Malcolm. But I have none: the king-becoming graces,
As justice, verity, temperance, stableness,
Bounty, perseverance, mercy, lowliness,
Devotion, patience, courage, fortitude,
I have no relish of them, but abound   95
In the division of each several crime,
Acting it many ways. Nay, had I power, I should
Pour the sweet milk of concord into hell,
Uproar the universal peace, confound
All unity on earth.

Macduff.   O Scotland, Scotland!   100

Malcolm. If such a one be fit to govern, speak:
I am as I have spoken.

Macduff.   Fit to govern!
No, not to live. O nation miserable,
With an untitled tyrant bloody-scepter'd,
When shalt thou see thy wholesome days again,   105
Since that the truest issue of thy throne
By his own interdiction stands accurs'd,
And does blaspheme his breed? Thy royal father
Was a most sainted king; the queen that bore thee,
Oft'ner upon her knees than on her feet,   110
Died every day she liv'd. Fare thee well!

88 **foisons:** plenty, abundance.   89 **your mere own:** wholly
yours.   89 **portable:** bearable.   90 **With . . . weigh'd:**
if balanced with, set over against.   95 **relish:** flavour, tinge.
96 **In the division of:** in all the different aspects of.   99–100
Uproar . . . earth: turn all peace and unity into confusion.   104
subject to the bloody rule of a usurper (with no title to the crown).
107 **his own interdiction:** exclusion of himself.   108 **blaspheme his breed:** casts a slur on his parentage (by confession of
his vices).   111 **Died . . . liv'd:** lived a life of daily abstinence
and self-sacrifice.

These evils thou repeat'st upon thyself
Have banish'd me from Scotland. O my breast,
Thy hope ends here!

  Malcolm.   Macduff, this noble passion,
Child of integrity, hath from my soul   115
Wip'd the black scruples, reconcil'd my thoughts
To thy good truth and honour. Devilish Macbeth
By many of these trains hath sought to win me
Into his power, and modest wisdom plucks me
From over-credulous haste; but God above   120
Deal between thee and me! for even now
I put myself to thy direction, and
Unspeak mine own detraction, here abjure
The taints and blames I laid upon myself,
For strangers to my nature. I am yet   125
Unknown to woman, never was forsworn,
Scarcely have coveted what was mine own;
At no time broke my faith, would not betray
The devil to his fellow, and delight
No less in truth than life; my first false speaking   130
Was this upon myself. What I am truly,
Is thine and my poor country's to command;
Whither indeed, before thy here-approach,
Old Siward, with ten thousand war-like men,
Already at a point, was setting forth.   135
Now we'll together, and the chance of goodness
Be like our warranted quarrel. Why are you silent?

  Macduff. Such welcome and unwelcome things at once
'Tis hard to reconcile.

112 **upon:** against (so in l. 131).   116 **black scruples:** dark
suspicions of l. 14, &c.   118 **trains:** stratagems.   119
modest: restraining, moderating.   121 **deal between thee
and me:** control our relations.   122 **to:** under.   126 **was
forsworn:** perjured myself.   135 **at a point:** in readiness.
136-7 **the chance . . . quarrel:** may the chance of success be as
certain as the justice of our cause [N].

Enter a Doctor.

Malcolm. Well; more anon. Comes the king forth, I pray
    you?   140
Doctor. Ay, sir; there are a crew of wretched souls
That stay his cure; their malady convinces
The great assay of art; but, at his touch,
Such sanctity hath heaven given his hand,
They presently amend.
Malcolm.   I thank you, doctor.   145
        [*Exit* Doctor.

Macduff. What's the disease he means?
Malcolm.   'Tis call'd the evil:
A most miraculous work in this good king,
Which often, since my here-remain in England,
I have seen him do. How he solicits heaven,
Himself best knows; but strangely-visited people,   150
All swoln and ulcerous, pitiful to the eye,
The mere despair of surgery, he cures,
Hanging a golden stamp about their necks,
Put on with holy prayers; and 'tis spoken,
To the succeeding royalty he leaves   155
The healing benediction. With this strange virtue,
He hath a heavenly gift of prophecy,
And sundry blessings hang about his throne
That speak him full of grace.
Macduff.   See, who comes here?
Malcolm. My countryman; but yet I know him not.   100

140 **the king** of England, Edward the Confessor.   142 **stay:**
await.   142–3 **convinces . . . art:** overcomes the greatest
effort of (medical) skill.   145 **presently:** immediately.   146 **evil:**
i.e. the king's evil, or scrofula.   149 **solicits:** prays (the help of).
150 **strangely-visited:** strangely afflicted.   152 **mere:** absolute,
utter.   153 **a golden stamp:** coin [*N*].   154 **spoken:** said.
156 **The healing benediction:** the blessed gift of healing.   **virtue:**
power.

Enter ROSS.

Macduff. My ever-gentle cousin, welcome hither.
Malcolm. I know him now. Good God, betimes remove
The means that makes us strangers!
Ross. Sir, amen.
Macduff. Stands Scotland where it did?
Ross. Alas! poor country;
Almost afraid to know itself. It cannot 165
Be call'd our mother, but our grave; where nothing,
But who knows nothing, is once seen to smile;
Where sighs and groans and shrieks that rent the air
Are made, not mark'd; where violent sorrow seems
A modern ecstasy; the dead man's knell 170
Is there scarce ask'd for who; and good men's lives
Expire before the flowers in their caps,
Dying or ere they sicken.
Macduff. O! relation
Too nice, and yet too true!
Malcolm. What's the newest grief?
Ross. That of an hour's age doth hiss the speaker; 175
Each minute teems a new one.
Macduff. How does my wife?
Ross. Why, well.
Macduff. And all my children?
Ross. Well too.
Macduff. The tyrant has not batter'd at their peace?
Ross. No; they were well at peace when I did leave 'em.
Macduff. Be not a niggard of your speech: how goes 't?

163 **means**: obstacle. 166 **nothing**: no one (but the expression is chosen to suggest that there can be no such living person).
168 **rent**: rend. 170 **modern ecstasy**: a perturbation of no
moment [*N*]. 170–1 **the dead man's . . . who**: no one
troubles to ask for whom the knell is rung. 173 **or ere**: before
[*N*]. 173–4 **relation Too nice**: record too elaborate. 175
i.e. the telling of a grief an hour old may cause the speaker to be
hissed for bringing stale news. 176 **teems**: produces.

Ross. When I came hither to transport the tidings,
Which I have heavily borne, there ran a rumour
Of many worthy fellows that were out;
Which was to my belief witness'd the rather
For that I saw the tyrant's power a-foot.   185
Now is the time of help; your eye in Scotland
Would create soldiers, make our women fight,
To doff their dire distresses.

    Malcolm.   Be 't their comfort
We are coming thither. Gracious England hath
Lent us good Siward and ten thousand men;   100
An older and a better soldier none
That Christendom gives out.

    Ross.   Would I could answer
This comfort with the like! But I have words
That would be howl'd out in the desert air,
Where hearing should not latch them.

    Macduff.   What concern they? 195
The general cause? or is it a fee-grief
Due to some single breast?

    Ross.   No mind that's honest
But in it shares some woe, though the main part
Pertains to you alone.

    Macduff.   If it be mine
Keep it not from me; quickly let me have it.   200

    Ross. Let not your ears despise my tongue for ever,
Which shall possess them with the heaviest sound
That ever yet they heard.

    Macduff.   Hum! I guess at it.

---

183 **out**: in the field (i.e against Macbeth).   185 **power**:
army.   186 **of help**: to bring help.   189 **England**: Cf. i. ii. 51, iv.
iii. 43.   191–2 **An older ... gives out**: none in Christendom is reputed an older or better soldier.   194 **would**: should.   195 **latch**:
catch. 196 **fee-grief**: private grief [*N*].   198 **in it ... woe**: has
some share in this grief.   202 **possess them with**: put them in
possession of.   203 **Hum**: any inarticulate sound of alarm is meant.

Ross. Your castle is surpris'd; your wife and babes
Savagely slaughter'd; to relate the manner,   205
Were, on the quarry of these murder'd deer,
To add the death of you.
Malcolm.   Merciful heaven!
What! man; ne'er pull your hat upon your brows;
Give sorrow words; the grief that does not speak
Whispers the o'er-fraught heart and bids it break.   210
  Macduff. My children too?
  Ross.   Wife, children, servants, all
That could be found.
  Macduff.   And I must be from thence!
My wife kill'd too?
  Ross.   I have said.
  Malcolm.   Be comforted:
Let's make us medicine of our great revenge,
To cure this deadly grief.   215
  Macduff. He has no children. All my pretty ones?
Did you say all? O hell-kite! All?
What! all my pretty chickens and their dam
At one fell swoop?
  Malcolm.   Dispute it like a man.
  Macduff.   I shall do so;
But I must also feel it as a man: 220
I cannot but remember such things were,
That were most precious to me. Did heaven look on,
And would not take their part? Sinful Macduff!
They were all struck for thee. Naught that I am,
Not for their own demerits, but for mine,   225
Fell slaughter on their souls. Heaven rest them now!

206 **quarry:** a heap of corpses. The full tale might add Macduff's
death to that of his family.   **210 whispers:** whispers to.
o'er-fraught: overburdened.   **212 and I ... thence:** and I had
to be away!   **214 of:** out of.   **216 He:** Macbeth (probably) [N].
219 Dispute it: resist it.   **224 Naught:** worthless creature.

Malcolm. Be this the whetstone of your sword: let grief
Convert to anger; blunt not the heart, enrage it.

Macduff. O! I could play the woman with mine eyes,
And braggart with my tongue. But, gentle heavens,   230
Cut short all intermission; front to front
Bring thou this fiend of Scotland and myself;
Within my sword's length set him; if he 'scape,
Heaven forgive him too!

Malcolm.   This tune goes manly.
Come, go we to the king; our power is ready;   235
Our lack is nothing but our leave. Macbeth
Is ripe for shaking, and the powers above
Put on their instruments. Receive what cheer you may;
The night is long that never finds the day.   [*Exeunt.*

228 **convert:** change (itself).   231 **intermission:** delay.
234 **This tune . . . manly:** this is a manly strain in which to speak.
236 **Our lack . . . leave:** nothing remains for us but to take our
leave.   237 **shaking:** i.e. punishment (metaphor from a tree).
237–8 **the powers . . . instruments:** Heaven is using Malcolm
and his supporters as its instruments.   238 **Put on:** urge on.

ACT V

Scene I. DUNSINANE. A ROOM IN THE CASTLE

Enter a Doctor of Physic *and a* Waiting-Gentlewoman.

Doctor. I have two nights watched with you, but can perceive no truth in your report. When was it she last walked? 3

Gentlewoman. Since his majesty went into the field, I have seen her rise from her bed, throw her night-gown upon her, unlock her closet, take forth paper, fold it, write upon 't, read it, afterwards seal it, and again return to bed; yet all this while in a most fast sleep. 8

Doctor. A great perturbation in nature, to receive at once the benefit of sleep and do the effects of watching! In this slumbery agitation, besides her walking and other actual performances, what, at any time, have you heard her say? 13

Gentlewoman. That, sir, which I will not report after her.

Doctor. You may to me, and 'tis most meet you should.

Gentlewoman. Neither to you nor any one, having no witness to confirm my speech.

Enter LADY MACBETH, *with a taper.*

Lo you! here she comes. This is her very guise; and, upon my life, fast asleep. Observe her; stand close.

Doctor. How came she by that light? 20

Gentlewoman. Why, it stood by her: she has light by her continually; 'tis her command.

2 **your report:** i.e. of her sleep-walking.   5 **night-gown:** cf. II. ii. 71.   10 **do . . . watching:** act as if awake.   12 **actual performances:** acts as distinguished from words.   14 **after her:** according to her words.   18 **This . . . guise:** this is the very way she has done it before.   19 **close:** concealed.

Doctor. You see, her eyes are open.

Gentlewoman. Ay, but their sense is shut.

Doctor. What is it she does now? Look, how she rubs her hands.   26

Gentlewoman. It is an accustomed action with her, to seem thus washing her hands. I have known her to continue in this a quarter of an hour.

Lady Macbeth. Yet here's a spot.   30

Doctor. Hark! she speaks. I will set down what comes from her, to satisfy my remembrance the more strongly.

Lady Macbeth. Out, damned spot! out, I say! One; two: why, then 'tis time to do 't. Hell is murky! Fie, my lord, fie! a soldier, and afeard? What need we 35 fear who knows it, when none can call our power to account? Yet who would have thought the old man to have had so much blood in him?

Doctor. Do you mark that?   39

Lady Macbeth. The Thane of Fife had a wife: where is she now? What! will these hands ne'er be clean? No more o' that, my lord, no more o' that: you mar all with this starting.

Doctor. Go to, go to; you have known what you should not.   45

Gentlewoman. She has spoke what she should not, I am sure of that: Heaven knows what she has known.

Lady Macbeth. Here's the smell of the blood still: all the perfumes of Arabia will not sweeten this little hand. Oh! oh! oh!   50

Doctor. What a sigh is there! The heart is sorely charged.

Gentlewoman. I would not have such a heart in my bosom for the dignity of the whole body.

Doctor. Well, well, well.

Gentlewoman. Pray God it be, sir.   55

30 **spot**: stain, mark.   40 **Thane of Fife**: Macduff.   53
for the dignity . . . body: i.e. even for the sake of being queen.

Doctor. This disease is beyond my practice: yet I have known those which have walked in their sleep who have died holily in their beds.

Lady Macbeth. Wash your hands, put on your night-gown; look not so pale. I tell you yet again, Banquo's buried; he cannot come out on 's grave.   61

Doctor. Even so?

Lady Macbeth. To bed, to bed: there's knocking at the gate. Come, come, come, come, give me your hand. What's done cannot be undone. To bed, to bed, to bed.   [*Exit.*

Doctor. Will she go now to bed?   66

Gentlewoman. Directly.

Doctor. Foul whisperings are abroad. Unnatural deeds
Do breed unnatural troubles; infected minds
To their deaf pillows will discharge their secrets;   70
More needs she the divine than the physician.
God, God forgive us all! Look after her;
Remove from her the means of all annoyance,
And still keep eyes upon her. So, good-night:
My mind she has mated, and amaz'd my sight.   75
I think, but dare not speak.

Gentlewoman.   Good-night, good doctor. [*Exeunt.*

Scene II. The Country near Dunsinane

*Enter, with drum and colours, MENTEITH, CAITHNESS,
ANGUS, LENNOX, and Soldiers.*

Menteith. The English power is near, led on by Malcolm,
His uncle Siward, and the good Macduff.
Revenges burn in them; for their dear causes

62 **Even so?** i.e. now I know all.   68 **whisperings:** rumours.
71 i.e. her soul needs medicine more than her body.   73 **means
of all annoyance:** all means of doing harm to herself.   75 **mated:**
confounded, overcome.   3 **revenges:** (plural) i.e. each has his
own desire for revenge.   **dear causes:** causes that touch them
closely.

Would to the bleeding and the grim alarm
Excite the mortified man.

  Angus.   Near Birnam wood   **5**
Shall we well meet them; that way are they coming.

  Caithness. Who knows if Donalbain be with his brother?

  Lennox. For certain, sir, he is not: I have a file
Of all the gentry: there is Siward's son,
And many unrough youths that even now   **10**
Protest their first of manhood.

  Menteith.   What does the tyrant?

  Caithness. Great Dunsinane he strongly fortifies.
Some say he's mad; others that lesser hate him
Do call it valiant fury; but, for certain,
He cannot buckle his distemper'd cause   **15**
Within the belt of rule.

  Angus.   Now does he feel
His secret murders sticking on his hands;
Now minutely revolts upbraid his faith-breach;
Those he commands move only in command,
Nothing in love; now does he feel his title   **20**
Hang loose about him, like a giant's robe
Upon a dwarfish thief.

  Menteith.   Who then shall blame
His pester'd senses to recoil and start,
When all that is within him does condemn
Itself for being there?

  Caithness.   Well, march we on,   **25**

4–5 **to the bleeding . . . man**: arouse even the ascetic to the grim summons to arms [*N*].   8 **file**: cf. III. i. 95.   10 **unrough**: smooth-chinned.   11 **Protest . . . manhood**: give the earliest proof that they have reached man's estate.   15–16 **He cannot . . . rule**: he cannot control his disorganized party [*N*].   17 **sticking . . . hands**: hampering him.   18 **minutely**: every minute.   20 **title**: kingship.   23 **pester'd**: bewildered. **to recoil**: for recoiling.   24–5 **When . . . there**: when all the faculties of the mind are employed in self-condemnation (Johnson).

To give obedience where 'tis truly ow'd;
Meet we the medicine of the sickly weal,
And with him pour we in our country's purge
Each drop of us.

Lennox.   Or so much as it needs
To dew the sovereign flower and drown the weeds.   30
Make we our march towards Birnam. [*Exeunt, marching.*

Scene III. DUNSINANE. A ROOM IN THE CASTLE

Enter MACBETH, Doctor, *and* Attendants.

Macbeth. Bring me no more reports; let them fly all:
Till Birnam wood remove to Dunsinane
I cannot taint with fear. What's the boy Malcolm?
Was he not born of woman? The spirits that know
All mortal consequences have pronounc'd me thus: 5
'Fear not, Macbeth; no man that's born of woman
Shall e'er have power upon thee.' Then fly, false thanes,
And mingle with the English epicures:
The mind I sway by and the heart I bear
Shall never sag with doubt nor shake with fear.   10

Enter a Servant.

The devil damn thee black, thou cream-fac'd loon!
Where gott'st thou that goose look?

Servant. There is ten thousand—

Macbeth.   Geese, villain?

Servant.   Soldiers, sir.

27 **the medicine:** physician, i.e. Malcolm, who was to heal the
state of its diseases. (Cf. IV. iii. 214) [*N*].   **the sickly weal:** the
diseased state or community.   28 **in our country's purge:** in
purging our country.   30 **dew:** water [*N*].   1 **let them fly
all:** let all my nobles desert me. Cf. l. 7 and v. ii. 18.   3 **taint:**
be tainted.   5 **All ... consequences:** the future of all human
affairs.   9 **sway by:** by which I rule.   10 **sag:** droop.   11
loon: lout.

Macbeth. Go, prick thy face, and over-red thy fear,
Thou lily-liver'd boy. What soldiers, patch?   15
Death of thy soul! those linen cheeks of thine
Are counsellors to fear. What soldiers, whey-face?
 Servant. The English force, so please you.
 Macbeth. Take thy face hence. [*Exit* Servant.] Seyton!
        —I am sick at heart
When I behold—Seyton, I say!—This push   20
Will cheer me ever or disseat me now.
I have liv'd long enough: my way of life
Is fall'n into the sear, the yellow leaf;
And that which should accompany old age,
As honour, love, obedience, troops of friends,   25
I must not look to have; but, in their stead,
Curses, not loud but deep, mouth-honour, breath,
Which the poor heart would fain deny, and dare not.
Seyton!
        29

Sympathy (margin annotation)

Enter SEYTON.

 Seyton. What is your gracious pleasure?
 Macbeth.   What news more?
 Seyton. All is confirm'd, my lord, which was reported.
 Macbeth. I'll fight till from my bones my flesh be hack'd.
Give me my armour.
 Seymour.   'Tis not needed yet.
 Macbeth. I'll put it on.
Send out more horses, skirr the country round;   35
Hang those that talk of fear. Give me mine armour.
How does your patient, doctor?
 Doctor.   Not so sick, my lord,

14 **prick . . . thy fear**: let the blood cover up thy white face.
15 **lily-liver'd**: cowardly [*N*].   **patch**: clown.   17 **Are counsellors to**: suggest.   20 **push**: sally, onset.   21 **cheer**:
comfort, encourage.   23 **sear**: i.e. sere: dry, withered [*N*].
27 **mouth-honour**: lip-service.   28 **deny**: withhold.   35
skirr: scour.

As she is troubled with thick-coming fancies,
That keep her from her rest.

Macbeth.   Cure her of that:
Canst thou not minister to a mind diseas'd,   40
Pluck from the memory a rooted sorrow,
Raze out the written troubles of the brain,
And with some sweet oblivious antidote
Cleanse the stuff'd bosom of that perilous stuff
Which weighs upon the heart?

Doctor.   Therein the patient   45
Must minister to himself.

Macbeth. Throw physic to the dogs; I'll none of it.
Come, put mine armour on; give me my staff.
Seyton, send out.—Doctor, the thanes fly from me.—
Come, sir, dispatch.—If thou couldst, doctor, cast   50
The water of my land, find her disease,
And purge it to a sound and pristine health,
I would applaud thee to the very echo,
That should applaud again.—Pull 't off, I say.—
What rhubarb, senna, or what purgative drug   55
Would scour these English hence? Hear'st thou of
      them?

Doctor. Ay, my good lord; your royal preparation
Makes us hear something.

Macbeth.   Bring it after me.
I will not be afraid of death and bane
Till Birnam forest come to Dunsinane.   60

Doctor. [*Aside.*] Were I from Dunsinane away and
      clear,
Profit again should hardly draw me here.   [*Exeunt.*

---

41 **rooted:** firm-fixed.   43 **oblivious:** causing forgetfulness.
48 **staff:** either general's baton, or spear-shaft.   50–1 **cast
the water of:** diagnose the condition of.   54 **Pull't off:** i.e. the
armour.   58 **it:** the armour (spoken to Seyton).   59 **bane:**
ruin, destruction.

Scene IV. COUNTRY NEAR BIRNAM WOOD

Enter, with drum and colours, MALCOLM, *Old* SIWARD
and his Son, MACDUFF, MENTEITH, CAITHNESS, ANGUS,
LENNOX, ROSS, *and* Soldiers *marching.*

Malcolm. Cousins, I hope the days are near at hand
That chambers will be safe.
  Menteith.   We doubt it nothing.
 Siward. What wood is this before us?
 Menteith. The wood of Birnam.
 Malcolm. Let every soldier hew him down a bough 5
And bear 't before him: thereby shall we shadow
The numbers of our host, and make discovery
Err in report of us.
 Soldiers.   It shall be done.
 Siward. We learn no other but the confident tyrant
Keeps still in Dunsinane, and will endure 10
Our setting down before 't.
 Malcolm.   'Tis his main hope;
For where there is advantage to be given,
Both more and less have given him the revolt,
And none serve with him but constrained things
Whose hearts are absent too.
 Macduff.   Let our just censures 15
Attend the true event, and put we on
Industrious soldiership.
 Siward.   The time approaches
That will with due decision make us know

---

2 **That chambers will be safe:** when a man can rest at home
without danger. 7 **discovery:** the enemy's scouts. 9
no other but: no otherwise than. 10–11 **endure . . . before
't:** stand a siege. 12 **to be given** (to them): i.e. open to them
[*N*]. 13 **more:** great. 15–16 **Let our just censures
. . . event:** let our judgements await the actual issue and so be just.
16–17 **put . . . soldiership:** take full military precautions.

What we shall say we have and what we owe.
Thoughts speculative their unsure hopes relate,   20
But certain issue strokes must arbitrate,
Towards which advance the war.

> [*Exeunt, marching.*

Scene V. DUNSINANE. WITHIN THE CASTLE

Enter, with a drum and colours, MACBETH, SEYTON,
and Soldiers.

Macbeth. Hang out our banners on the outward walls;
The cry is still, 'They come;' our castle's strength
Will laugh a siege to scorn; here let them lie
Till famine and the ague eat them up;
Were they not forc'd with those that should be ours,   5
We might have met them dareful, beard to beard,
And beat them backward home.

> [*A cry of women within.*
> What is that noise?

Seyton. It is the cry of women, my good lord.   [*Exit.*
Macbeth. I have almost forgot the taste of fears.
The time has been my senses would have cool'd   10
To hear a night-shriek, and my fell of hair
Would at a dismal treatise rouse and stir
As life were in 't. I have supp'd full with horrors;
Direness, familiar to my slaughterous thoughts,
Cannot once start me.

Re-enter SEYTON.

> Wherefore was that cry?   15
Seyton. The queen, my lord, is dead.

19 **what we owe:** i.e. what we have lost; i.e. our gains and losses.
20 i.e. surmises offer uncertain hopes (scan spec(u)lative).   21
arbitrate: settle, determine.   5 **forc'd:** reinforced.   6 **dareful:** darefully, i.e. in a (more) daring way.   10 **my senses . . . cool'd:** I should have felt a cold shiver.   11 **fell of hair:** scalp with hair on it (fell = skin).   12 **treatise:** tale.

Macbeth. She should have died hereafter;
There would have been a time for such a word.
To-morrow, and to-morrow, and to-morrow,
Creeps in this petty pace from day to day,   20
To the last syllable of recorded time;
And all our yesterdays have lighted fools
The way to dusty death. Out, out, brief candle!
Life's but a walking shadow, a poor player
That struts and frets his hour upon the stage,   25
And then is heard no more; it is a tale
Told by an idiot, full of sound and fury,
Signifying nothing.

Enter a Messenger.

Thou com'st to use thy tongue; thy story quickly.
    Messenger. Gracious my lord,   30
I should report that which I say I saw,
But know not how to do it.
    Macbeth.   Well, say, sir.
    Messenger. As I did stand my watch upon the hill,
I look'd towards Birnam, and anon, methought,
The wood began to move.
    Macbeth.   Liar and slave!   35
    Messenger. Let me endure your wrath if 't be not so:
Within this three mile you may see it coming;
I say, a moving grove.
    Macbeth.   If thou speak'st false,
Upon the next tree shalt thou hang alive,
Till famine cling thee; if thy speech be sooth,   40
I care not if thou dost for me as much.
I pull in resolution and begin
To doubt the equivocation of the fiend

18 **such a word:** such news [*N*].   34 **anon:** presently.   40
cling: shrivel up.   42 **pull in:** rein in.   43 **equivocation:**
cf. II. iii. 8–9.

That lies like truth; ' Fear not, till Birnam wood
Do come to Dunsinane;' and now a wood   45
Comes toward Dunsinane. Arm, arm, and out!
If this which he avouches does appear,
There is nor flying hence, nor tarrying here.
I 'gin to be aweary of the sun,
And wish the estate o' the world were now undone.   50
Ring the alarum-bell! Blow, wind! come, wrack!
At least we'll die with harness on our back.   [*Exeunt.*

Scene VI. THE SAME. A PLAIN BEFORE THE
CASTLE

Enter, with drum and colours, MALCOLM, *Old* SIWARD,
MACDUFF, *&c., and their Army, with boughs.*

Malcolm. Now near enough; your leavy screens throw
      down,
And show like those you are. You, worthy uncle,
Shall, with my cousin, your right-noble son,
Lead our first battle; worthy Macduff and we
Shall take upon 's what else remains to do,   5
According to our order.
   Siward.   Fare you well.
Do we but find the tyrant's power to-night,
Let us be beaten, if we cannot fight.
   Macduff. Make all our trumpets speak; give them all
      breath,
Those clamorous harbingers of blood and death.   10
                                              [*Exeunt.*

50 **estate:** settled condition.   51 **wrack:** See I. i. 26.   52
harness: armour.   2 **show:** appear.   **uncle:** i.e. Siward.
4 **battle:** division of an army.   7 **Do we but:** if we only.
power: forces.

Scene VII. The Same. Another Part of the Plain

Alarums. Enter MACBETH.

Macbeth. They have tied me to a stake; I cannot fly,
But bear-like I must fight the course. What's he
That was not born of woman? Such a one
Am I to fear, or none.

Enter Young SIWARD.

Young Siward. What is thy name?
Macbeth.   Thou'lt be afraid to hear it. 5
Young Siward. No; though thou call'st thyself a hotter name
Than any is in hell.
Macbeth.   My name's Macbeth.
Young Siward. The devil himself could not pronounce a title
More hateful to mine ear.
Macbeth.   No, nor more fearful.
Young Siward. Thou liest, abhorred tyrant; with my sword   10
I'll prove the lie thou speak'st.
                    [*They fight and Young* SIWARD *is slain.*
Macbeth.   Thou wast born of woman:
But swords I smile at, weapons laugh to scorn,
Brandish'd by man that's of a woman born.   [*Exit.*

Alarums. Enter MACDUFF.

Macduff. That way the noise is. Tyrant, show thy face:
If thou be'st slain and with no stroke of mine,   15
My wife and children's ghosts will haunt me still.
I cannot strike at wretched kerns, whose arms

2 **course:** the name in bear-baiting for the attack of the dogs.
17 **kerns:** cf. i. ii. 13; but here used as a contemptuous term for 'boors'.

Are hir'd to bear their staves: either thou, Macbeth,
Or else my sword with an unbatter'd edge
I sheathe again undeeded. There thou shouldst be;   20
By this great clatter, one of greatest note
Seems bruited. Let me find him, fortune!
And more I beg not.   [*Exit. Alarums.*

Enter MALCOLM *and Old* SIWARD.

Siward. This way, my lord; the castle's gently render'd:
The tyrant's people on both sides do fight;   25
The noble thanes do bravely in the war;
The day almost itself professes yours,
And little is to do.
Malcolm.   We have met with foes
That strike beside us.
Siward.   Enter, sir, the castle. [*Exeunt. Alarums.*

Re-enter MACBETH.

Macbeth. Why should I play the Roman fool, and die
On mine own sword? whiles I see lives, the gashes   31
Do better upon them.

Re-enter MACDUFF.

Macduff.   Turn, hell-hound, turn!
Macbeth. Of all men else I have avoided thee:
But get thee back, my soul is too much charg'd
With blood of thine already.
Macduff.   I have no words;   35
My voice is in my sword, thou bloodier villain

18 **staves:** spear-shafts.   **either thou, Macbeth** (sc. must fight
me).   20 **undeeded:** without having done anything.   22
bruited: announced (by the noise).   24 **gently:** without resistance.   25 i.e. some of Macbeth's men have deserted
to us.   29 **beside us:** i.e. beside the mark, so as to miss us.
31 **lives:** living enemies.   33 **Of all men else:** more than
all others.

Than terms can give thee out!   [*They fight.*

    Macbeth.   Thou losest labour:
As easy mayst thou the intrenchant air
With thy keen sword impress as make me bleed:
Let fall thy blade on vulnerable crests;   40
I bear a charmed life, which must not yield
To one of woman born.

    Macduff.   Despair thy charm;
And let the angel whom thou still hast serv'd
Tell thee, Macduff was from his mother's womb
Untimely ripp'd.   45

    Macbeth. Accursed be that tongue that tells me so,
For it hath cow'd my better part of man:
And be these juggling fiends no more believ'd,
That palter with us in a double sense;
That keep the word of promise to our ear,   50
And break it to our hope. I'll not fight with thee.

    Macduff. Then yield thee, coward,
And live to be the show and gaze o' the time:
We'll have thee, as our rarer monsters are,
Painted upon a pole, and underwrit,   55
'Here may you see the tyrant.'

    Macbeth.   I will not yield,
To kiss the ground before young Malcolm's feet,
And to be baited with the rabble's curse.
Though Birnam wood be come to Dunsinane,
And thou oppos'd, being of no woman born,   60

---

37 **terms**: words, expressions.   38 **intrenchant**: literally, not
cutting; here = not to be cut, invulnerable (cf. III. iv. 27).   42
Despair: despair of.   **charm**: charmed life.   43 **angel**: evil
angel.   **still**: ever.   45 **Untimely**: prematurely.   47 **my
better part of man**: i.e. my manliness [*N*].   49 **palter**:
quibble, trifle.   53 **gaze o' the time**: gazing stock, sight of the
day.   55 **underwrit**: we will have written below [*N*].   58
baited: like a bear by dogs: cf. v. vii. 2.   60 **oppos'd**: set
against me.

Yet I will try the last: before my body
I throw my war-like shield. Lay on, Macduff,
And damn'd be him that first cries, 'Hold, enough!'

[*Exeunt, fighting.*

Retreat. Flourish. Re-enter, with drum and colours,
MALCOLM, *Old* SIWARD, ROSS, Thanes, *and* Soldiers.

Malcolm. I would the friends we miss were safe arriv'd.

Siward. Some must go off; and yet, by these I see,   65
So great a day as this is cheaply bought.

Malcolm. Macduff is missing, and your noble son.

Ross. Your son, my lord, has paid a soldier's debt:
He only liv'd but till he was a man;
The which no sooner had his prowess confirm'd   70
In the unshrinking station where he fought,
But like a man he died.

Siward.   Then he is dead?

Ross. Ay, and brought off the field. Your cause of sorrow
Must not be measur'd by his worth, for then
It hath no end.

Siward.   Had he his hurts before?   75

Ross. Ay, on the front.

Siward.   Why then, God's soldier be he!
Had I as many sons as I have hairs,
I would not wish them to a fairer death:
And so, his knell is knoll'd.

Malcolm.   He's worth more sorrow,
And that I'll spend for him.

Siward.   He's worth no more;   80
They say he parted well, and paid his score:
And so, God be with him! Here comes newer comfort.

65 **go off**: be killed (a euphemism).   **by these I see**: considering
these who I see have survived.   71 **In the unshrinking station
. . . fought**: in the post where he fought without shrinking.   81
he parted well, and paid his score: he departed well (as from an
inn) and paid his reckoning.

Re-enter MACDUFF, *with* MACBETH'S *head.*

Macduff. Hail, king! for so thou art. Behold, where
    stands
The usurper's cursed head: the time is free:
I see thee compass'd with thy kingdom's pearl,   85
That speak my salutation in their minds;
Whose voices I desire aloud with mine;
Hail, King of Scotland!
   All.   Hail, King of Scotland!
                                  [Flourish.
   Malcolm. We shall not spend a large expense of time
Before we reckon with your several loves,   90
And make us even with you. My thanes and kinsmen,
Henceforth be earls, the first that ever Scotland
In such an honour nam'd. What's more to do,
Which would be planted newly with the time,
As calling home our exil'd friends abroad   95
That fled the snares of watchful tyranny;
Producing forth the cruel ministers
Of this dead butcher and his fiend-like queen,
Who, as 'tis thought, by self and violent hands
Took off her life; this, and what needful else   100
That calls upon us, by the grace of Grace
We will perform in measure, time, and place:
So, thanks to all at once and to each one,
Whom we invite to see us crown'd at Scone.
                          [Flourish. Exeunt.

  84 **the time is free:** the age is delivered.   85 **compass'd
with thy kingdom's pearl:** surrounded with the 'flower' of thy
kingdom.   90 **your several loves:** the love of each of you.
91 **even with you:** i.e. by rewarding you for your services.   92–3
the first . . . nam'd: the first of that title in Scotland [*N*]. 94
would: should.   95 **as:** such as.   97 **Producing forth:**
bringing to justice.   99 **by self . . . hands:** by doing herself
violence.   101 **by the grace of Grace:** i.e. of God.

NOTES

Folio = First Folio of 1623.

References to other plays are made to the one volume Oxford Shakespeare.

Textual notes and some other more advanced notes are enclosed within brackets, thus [ ].

Some of the most obvious metrical difficulties are explained, but no attempt is made to deal with every irregularity. See Appendix III.

ACT I. Scene I

One of the most striking plunges *in medias res* even in Shakespeare. In a dozen lines the keynote of the play is struck: the three Witches, 'the instruments of darkness' (I. iii. 124), awaiting the issue of battle, make their appointment to meet Macbeth on the heath.

8. Graymalkin was a common name for a grey cat.

9. Paddock means 'toad'.

11. A significant incantation. The Witches stand for those who have said 'Evil, be thou my good', who have destroyed the distinction of 'foul and fair'.

ACT I. Scene II

This scene gives us a strong idea of Macbeth's *bravery*. A Sergeant straight from the battle-field informs the King, in a few breathless sentences, that the issue between the loyal Macbeth and the rebellious Macdonwald still hangs in the balance. A moment later it is announced by Ross that Macbeth is victorious.

[For 'Sergeant' Folio has 'Captaine' in stage-direction, but the text (l. 3) justifies the change.]

[The abruptness of the style in this scene has led some critics to suppose that it is from another hand. Writing of a similar kind, however, occurs in other plays of Shakespeare, e.g. in the Player's recitation in *Hamlet* (II. ii). This special style may be described as Shakespeare's *epic* as contrasted with his normal dramatic manner. One of its features is the use of picturesque similes (see ll. 8, 9; 25–8; 35–7); another is the harsh energy of the rhythms. The purpose of the style in *Macbeth* I. ii seems to be to raise the level of the drama to a heroic plane as rapidly as possible.]

5. [Some think that 'hail' is to be scanned as two syllables. More probably the line is like several others, in *Macbeth*, in which a single syllable, after a marked pause, counts as a whole foot. In that case, the scansion would be:

'Gainst my | captiv|ity. || Hail, | brave friend! | See A Note on Metre, Note 2.]

7. [The omission of syllable a may be attributed to the marked pause consequent on the division of the line between two speakers.]

9. **choke their art.** A compressed phrase suggesting that the tired swimmers, clutching each other, render their skill useless, and choke each other.

14. ['Quarrell' is Hanmer's correction of Folio 'Quarry'.]

16 **brave Macbeth.** Notice the numerous terms of praise which are lavished on Macbeth in the first Act of the Tragedy; e.g. 'Bellona's bridegroom' (ii. 55), 'noble Macbeth' (ii. 69), 'my noble partner' (iii. 54), 'most worthy thane' (iii. 106), 'worthy Macbeth' (iii. 148), 'worthiest cousin' (iv. 14), 'my worthy Cawdor' (iv. 47). Macbeth is thus vividly presented to our eyes as a hero; but the chorus of praise also contributes to the irony of the play (see note on I. iii. 38), for the hero of Act I becomes the 'tyrant' of Acts III–v. (See note on III. vi. 22.)

18. [Scan execut-i-on: five syllables. Shakespeare follows no rule for the termination -ion: sometimes it counts as one, sometimes as two syllables. Cf. 'reflection' in l. 25, and see Appendix III.]

20–1. Most editors agree that there is some corruption of the text here. The best way to understand l. 21 is to assume that some words are missing in l. 20 and that 'Macbeth' is the antecedent of 'which' (l. 21).

24. According to Holinshed, Duncan and Macbeth were the grandsons of Malcolm, King of Scotland, and the sons of his two daughters, Beatrice and Doada, respectively.

31–2. [Shakespeare does not here follow Holinshed closely, but compresses several events into one for dramatic effect. According to Holinshed 'Makdowald' is defeated by Macbeth and then commits suicide. Shortly after 'woord came that Sueno King of Norway was arriued in Fife with a puissant armie, to subdue the whole realme of Scotland'. Sueno is defeated, and then again 'woord was brought that a new fleet of Danes was arriued at Kingcorne, sent thither by Canute king of England, in reuenge of his brother Suenos ouerthrow'.]

34. [*captains* is perhaps to be scanned as three syllables; cf. Fr. *capitaine*. Cf. 3 *Henry VI*, IV. vii. 30, 'A wise stout captain, and soon persuaded.']

40. Blood begins already to dominate the play.

41. **Golgotha:** 'a place called Golgotha, that is to say, a place of a skull'. (St. Matthew xxvii. 33.)

55. **Bellona** was the Roman goddess of war.

63. **Colme's** is scanned as two syllables. 'Saint Colme's inch' is 'the island of St. Columba'. It is in the Firth of Forth and is now called Inchcolm. St. Columba was the first teacher of Christianity to the Picts.

64. **dollars:** an anachronism, of course. Dollars were first coined in the sixteenth century.

ACT I. Scene III

The three Witches, meeting on the heath according to their plan, are accosted by Macbeth and Banquo. They address Macbeth in a threefold greeting: Thane of Glamis, Thane of Cawdor, and 'king hereafter'. Banquo also receives a promise: though never to be a king himself, he is to be the ancestor of kings. Scarcely have the Witches disappeared, when news is brought to Macbeth that he is created Thane of Cawdor. The fulfilment of one prophecy brings the prospect of kingship vividly before Macbeth's eyes, but with it comes an image of horror which leaves him dead to his surroundings. With an effort he rouses himself, and accompanies the other nobles to the king.

7. **Tiger:** a fairly common name for a ship. Cf. *Twelfth Night*: 'And this is he that did the Tiger board' (v. i. 66).

8. 'He sits like a witch sailing in a sieve' (D'Avenant, *The Tragedy of Albovine*). It was also believed that witches 'could sail in an egg shell, a cockle or muscle shell, through and under the tempestuous seas' (Scot, *Discovery of Witchcraft*, 1584).

9. 'It should be remembered (as it was the belief of the times) that though a witch could assume the form of any animal she pleased, the tail would still be wanting' (Steevens).

20. **pent-house:** a building with a sloping roof, or a sloping roof itself.

32. **weird:** originally a noun meaning 'fate'. In *Macbeth* it is adjectival and means 'connected with fate, or destiny'.

> [Folio has 'weyward', i.e. 'weird' here; elsewhere 'wayward' which is etymologically quite distinct and occurs in its usual meaning in III. v. 11 'wayward son'. Theobald emended to 'weird' from Holinshed who uses the phrase 'weird sisters'.]

s.d. *Enter Macbeth and Banquo.* The contrast between the ways in which Macbeth and Banquo are severally affected by the Witches corresponds to the difference between guilt and innocence. Macbeth has already contemplated the murder of Duncan (see I. v. 1–30, I. vii. 47–52), and there is thus an understanding between him and 'the instruments of darkness'.

38. **So foul and fair a day . . .** Macbeth unconsciously echoes the words of the Witches (I. i. 11). This is an example of 'tragic irony': the saying of Macbeth has a double significance which is perceived by the spectators, but not by the speaker. 'Irony', in its various forms, is one of the most striking characteristics of this tragedy. Cf. I. iv. 14, I. vi. 1–3. (See Select Literary Criticism.)

48–50. The Witches' Salutations are taken from Holinshed, but Shakespeare increases their effect by making them take place at the very moment when Macbeth is flushed with victory, instead of a little time after the Norwegian invasions, as they are in Holinshed.

48. **Glamis** is said to be always pronounced in Scotland as a monosyllable. In some lines of this play, e.g. I. v. 14, I. v. 53, II. ii. 43, it certainly counts as a disyllable.

72–3. **the Thane of Cawdor lives, A prosperous gentleman.** Dr. Johnson asks: 'How can Macbeth be ignorant of the state of the Thane whom he has just defeated and taken prisoner, or call him a "prosperous gentleman" who has forfeited his title and life by open rebellion?' No really satisfactory answer has yet been given to this question. Some critics make the difficulty support their view that Scene ii of this Act is not wholly, or at all, the work of Shakespeare. Another theory is that Macbeth feigns ignorance to test the knowledge of the Witches and perhaps spur them on to say more about the prophecy of kingship. The second suggestion is attractive; yet it seems probable that if Shakespeare was making Macbeth test the knowledge of the Witches, he would have given some clearer indication of this in the text. The difficulty would be removed if I. iii. 112–13 means that Cawdor's assistance was secret, and that he himself was not present at the battle. In that case he might have continued to live as a prosperous gentleman for some time after Macbeth's victory. But lines I. ii. 51–8 scarcely seem to mean that Cawdor fought only by proxy.

84. [**insane:** accent the first syllable. Cf. II. iii. 41.]

107. [scan **devil** as one syllable. Cf. Scots 'deil'.]

111. [**Whether.** Scan 'whe'er'.]

120. [**trusted home.** The word 'home' in this phrase comes to mean 'completely' or 'thoroughly' by an extension of the sense which it has in a saying like 'the blow went home', i.e. 'went to its destined place, did its business thoroughly'. Cf. 'I will punish home', *King Lear*, III. iv. 16.]

127–42, 143–4, 146–7. All the soliloquies of Macbeth deserve the most careful study: they are great poetry (the finest in the play), and they are, naturally, the chief clue to his character. This particular speech raises the important question of Macbeth's relation to supernatural powers. The view taken by A. C. Bradley on this point is undoubtedly the true one: 'While the influence of the Witches' prophecies on Macbeth is very great, it is quite clearly shown to be an influence and nothing more. There is no sign whatever in the play that Shakespeare meant the actions of Macbeth to be forced on him by an external power, whether that of the Witches, or of their "masters", or of Hecate. It is needless therefore to insist that such a conception would be in contradiction with his whole tragic practice. . . . We are admitting too much when we use the word "temptation" in reference to the first prophecies of the Witches. Speaking strictly we must affirm that he was tempted only by himself. *He* speaks indeed of their "supernatural soliciting"; but in fact they did not solicit. They merely announced events: they hailed him as Thane of Glamis, Thane of Cawdor, and King hereafter. No connexion of these announcements with any action of his was even hinted by them. For all that appears, the natural death of an old man might have fulfilled the prophecy any day. In any case, the idea of fulfilling it by murder was entirely his own.'

129, 139. [See Note at the end of Appendix III.]

140. **single state of man.** (*a*) If 'single' has the sense 'unified' or 'harmonious', the meaning is 'the normal harmony of my commonwealth'. (*b*) If 'single' has the obsolete sense 'slight, poor, trivial', as in I. vi. 16, the meaning is 'my poor human realm' or 'the poor kingdom of my being'. Cf. Brutus's description of a man's condition 'between the acting of a dreadful thing And the first motion':

> the state of man,
> Like to a little kingdom, suffers then
> The nature of an insurrection. (*Julius Caesar*, II. i. 67–9).

147. **Time and the hour . . . day.** 'Time and the hour' was a proverbial expression for 'the lapse of time'. 'Runs through' has here the sense 'gets rid of'; (cf. 'he runs through his money'). Hence the line means: 'the most tempestuous day has its ending.'

ACT I. Scene IV

Duncan briefly expresses his gratitude to Macbeth, and honours
him by announcing a royal visit to his Castle. At the same time he
gives to Malcolm the title of Prince of Cumberland, thus designating
him heir-apparent, and creating an apparent obstacle to Macbeth's
hopes of the crown.

14. *Enter Macbeth,* &c. The entrance of Macbeth, immediately after
    Duncan's description of the traitor Cawdor 'a gentleman on whom
    I built An absolute trust', is a striking instance of Dramatic Irony,
    and the impression is deepened by Duncan's praise of Macbeth
    in the rest of the speech, and at intervals through the whole
    scene. (Cf. l. 58.)

ACT I. Scene V

In this scene the dramatic tension suddenly increases. We see at
a glance that Lady Macbeth is to play a major part in the action.
Hearing of the Witches' prophecy, she resolves that, despite any
scruples in her husband's mind, it shall be fulfilled. When, a moment
later, the Messenger appears with the news that Duncan will arrive
at the Castle that same night, she is staggered for an instant, but
at once recovering, decides that the time for action has come. On
Macbeth's entrance, few words are necessary: the two understand
each other completely, but the lead now passes into the hands of
Lady Macbeth.

18–19. **Art not without ambition . . . attend it.** Ambition is
    frequently spoken of by Shakespeare as a dangerous or evil
    quality. Cf. the words of Brutus: 'as he was ambitious, I slew
    him' (*Julius Caesar*, III. ii. 28–9), and of Wolsey: Cromwell,
    I charge thee, fling away ambition' (*Henry the Eighth*, III. ii. 441).

30–2. Lady Macbeth is taken aback by the sudden news, but tries
    to cover her surprise by suggesting a plausible reason for it (ll.
    31–2).

37. **The raven himself is hoarse . . .** The breathless messenger
    was hoarse (ll. 35–6); and the raven, with the fatal announcement
    which he makes, has good cause to be hoarse also.

47. Either 'Take my milk as if it were gall to feed you now that I
    am unsexed' (l. 40), or 'Take away my woman's milk and give me
    gall instead'.

54. the all-hail hereafter. It has been remarked that 'Lady Macbeth speaks as if she had heard the words as spoken by the witch, I. iii. 50, and not merely read them as reported in her husband's letter, I. v. 8, 9'. 'All-hail' is here an adjective. Shakespeare bends language to his need.

60. [The short line suggests that Lady Macbeth dismisses the matter abruptly and confidently.]

66. provided for. *Macbeth* is nearly as remarkable for its euphemisms as it is for its irony; cf. 'taking-off' (I. vii. 20) and 'quell' (I. vii. 72), both euphemisms for 'murder'. Lady Macbeth's 'provided for' is a particularly ghastly example.

ACT I. SCENE VI

The note of serene beauty on which this scene opens is unique in the play. Its dramatic purpose is to point the contrast between the unsuspecting confidence with which Duncan enters the Castle, and the dreadful purpose lurking beneath the hypocritical welcome of his hostess. Duncan's praise of the Castle in which he is to meet his end, and his frank greeting of Lady Macbeth, are striking examples of Dramatic Irony.

4. [There has been much discussion as to what bird is meant by the 'martlet', but the question seems to be settled by Gilbert White, who alludes to 'the house-martin, or martlet'. White's description of the 'house-martin' (*The Natural History of Selborne*, Letter LV) closely resembles Shakespeare's description of the 'martlet'.]

5. [mansionry: Folio has 'mansonry'; this *may* be only a misprint for 'masonry', not a Shakespearian coinage from 'mansion'.]

11–12. The love that follows us . . . love. Just as 'The love of our subjects ("that follows us") sometimes causes us "trouble", but our gratitude is none the less due to such love', so Duncan's visit to Lady Macbeth is no doubt a source of trouble to her (cf. l. 11), but it is also a proof of his own love; therefore, he says, she should be grateful for it.

13 'eyld, a form of 'yield', in its (now obsolete) sense of 'requite'.

ACT I. SCENE VII

An intensely critical scene. Macbeth, hesitating at the last moment on the brink of his crime, is met by the concentrated will of his wife, who, summoning up every means of appeal, in a few passionate sentences overcomes his resistance, and identifies herself irrevocably with the deed.

1–12. 'If the act were wholly finished when it is done, then it were well to perform it at once: if the act of murder could entangle its own results and obtain, at its conclusion, its object, so that this blow might be the one necessary stroke and end the business in this life—just in this life, this little bank of time in the sea of eternity, I would hazard the life to come. But in such cases, we always receive judgement even in this world, in that we merely teach others to do as we have done and are punished by our own example. This impartial operation of justice offers the cup which we have poisoned to our own lips.'

6. [shoal: Theobald's emendation of Folio 'schoole'.]

12–28. 'He has two reasons for feeling confidence in being here: first, because I am his kinsman and his subject, both of which relations are strong motives against the crime; next, because I am his host, whose part it is to protect him from murder, not execute it myself. Besides, this Duncan has exercised his powers with such moderation, has been so irreproachable in his great office, that his virtues will plead with the trumpet-like tongues of angels against the unforgivable crime of his murder; and pity, like a naked new-born baby riding on the blast, or the cherubin of heaven mounted on the invisible winds, will so present the horrible crime to the eyes of men that the flood of tears shall cause the wind to fall. I have no motive to instigate me but an excessive ambition, which leaps beyond its mark and falls on the other side.'

20. taking-off: a euphemism for 'murder'. See note on I. v. 66.

21. like a naked new-born babe: an image of innocence and helplessness.

22. [cherubin. Though elsewhere in Shakespeare 'cherubin' is singular (cf. *The Tempest*, I. ii. 152), here it is plural, but 'cherubim' (as in *Paradise Lost*, vi. 102) is a more correct form.]

25. That tears . . . wind: 'alluding to the remission of wind in a shower' (Johnson).

35–6. Was the hope . . . yourself? A clear indication, with ll. 47–9, that Macbeth had contemplated his plot before the beginning of the action in the play. Lady Macbeth takes up his metaphor from clothes (l. 34).

35–8. 'I cannot understand such a hope unless it was the result of drunkenness? Has it been asleep in the interval? And does it wake, sickly and frightened, to stare aghast at what it did of its freewill?'

45. **the poor cat i' the adage** was fond of fish, but did not like wetting its paws. The Low Latin form of the proverb was: 'catus amat pisces sed non vult tingere plantas.'

54–5. These lines, and the allusion to her father (II. ii. 14, 15) prove that Lady Macbeth is not utterly inhuman. In spite of her fanatical zeal for her husband's 'greatness', she has some feeling for others.

59. [**We fail?** 'Surely the usual interpretation of "We fail?" as a question of contemptuous astonishment, is right. "We fail!" gives practically the same sense, but alters the punctuation of the first two Folios. In either case, "But", I think, means "Only". On the other hand the proposal to read "We fail." with a full stop, as expressive of sublime acceptance of the possibility, seems to me, however attractive at first sight, quite out of harmony with Lady Macbeth's mood throughout these scenes.' (A. C. Bradley.)]

63 **chamberlains.** Not servants, probably, but court-officials. Later they are called 'grooms' (II. ii. 6) again not in the modern sense but in that occurring in 'Groom of the Chamber', 'Groom of the Stole', &c.

75–9. Notice that the murder of the grooms was not contemplated. Both Macbeth and Lady Macbeth *intended* a single crime, though Macbeth at any rate doubted whether one 'blow' could be the 'end-all' of the business (vii. 4, 5).

ACT II. Scene I

This short scene vividly suggests the moment of suspense before a crime is committed; it also throws a strong light on the changing character of Macbeth. All hesitation has now vanished, and he has even enough self-possession to hint to Banquo that his mind is set on self-advancement. When left alone, he shows no flinching of the will, however violent the terrors of his imagination. Notice how quickly the crisis comes in this tragedy as compared with *Hamlet, Othello*, and *King Lear*, in each of which it does not develop until the Third Act.

8–9. **Restrain in me the cursed thoughts that nature Gives way to in repose.** The meaning of this sentence is completed and illustrated by l. 20: 'I dreamt last night of the three weird Sisters.'

25. Macbeth's vagueness is deliberate. The *it* of '*tis* cannot be referred to any particular noun.

41. **As this which now I draw.** 'Macbeth may be supposed to draw his dagger after this short line' (Abbott).

50–6. The imagery is ghastly and exaggerated, as if Macbeth was compelling himself to realise 'the present horror'.

52. Hecate was a goddess of the underworld to whom witches were supposed to celebrate their rites. The name is scanned as two syllables, as often in Shakespeare. Cf. III. ii. 41, III. v. 1.

55. Tarquin. The story of Tarquin (i.e. Sextus Tarquinius) is told in Shakespeare's *Lucrece*. He was the ravisher of Lucretia; hence 'ravishing strides'.

61. [gives. The apparently singular form may be due to the attraction of the *sense* (i.e. 'words', plural = 'speech', singular), or the verb may have been influenced by the nearest noun, viz. 'breath'. An explanation more favourable to the grammar is that the -s represents the -es of the Northern dialect of Middle English, -es being the correct termination of the present indicative tense, third person plural. Shakespeare uses this form elsewhere; here he may have chosen it for the *rhyme*.]

ACT II. SCENE II

This scene is written in words of fire; further comment appears impossible.

5. The hooting of the owl was commonly supposed to portend death.

14–15. See note on I. vii. 54–5.

29. Macbeth is thinking of the hideous duties of the hangman at the execution of a traitor.

30. Listening: transitive. Cf. 'And now, Octavius, Listen great things'. (*Julius Caesar*, IV. i. 40–1.)

38. Sleep that knits up . . . The agitation of the moment puts Macbeth's imagination out of all control, and he expresses himself, as poets sometimes do, in a stream of metaphors. Cf. Henry Vaughan's poem *The Night*, ll. 25–8:

> Dear night! this world's defeat;
> The stop to busy fools; care's check and curb;
> The day of Spirits; my soul's calm retreat
> Which none disturb! &c.

55–6. 'tis the eye of childhood That fears a painted devil. Only children fear pictures of the devil. Cf. Webster's *Vittoria Corombona* (1612): 'Terrify babes, my lord, with painted devils.'

57. I'll gild the faces of the grooms withal. Shakespeare uses the verb 'gild' with many shades of meaning; in the tragedies, its suggestions are often evil or sinister: cf. 'This *gilded* serpent' (Albany of Goneril, *King Lear*, v. iii. 85), 'The *gilded* puddle which beasts would cough at' (*Antony and Cleopatra*, I. iv. 62–3). The sense of the word and its suggestions vary with the context. Here the word conveys a vague horror rather than a precise meaning; there is also a quibble with 'guilt' in the next line.

gild. Blood is also regarded as golden in II. iii. 95: 'His silver skin lac'd with his golden blood.'

64. [**green one red**: not, as in Folio, 'green one, red'.]

ACT II. Scene III

To introduce the buffoonery of the Porter after the intense drama of the preceding scene is an instance of extreme boldness—so extreme that S. T. Coleridge believed the Porter's speeches 'to have been written for the mob by some other hand'. Yet the contrast between Scenes ii and iii 1–20 is so handled that nothing of the preceding effect is lost; rather, a natural bridge between two great situations is provided. For one point of the Porter's speech is its unconscious irony: 'If a man were porter of hell-gate'—what is he but that, without knowing it? The manner in which Macbeth and Lady Macbeth act on the discovery of the murder shows that they have steeled themselves to meet the ordeal and are strong enough to make a plausible show of grief and horror. Macbeth does not lose control of the situation: his last act is to make a recommendation which is accepted unanimously (ll. 118–19). In the crisis no one seems to heed the king's youthful sons; they decide to slip away from the country, and bide their time, leaving a clear field for Macbeth meanwhile.

4–5. **Here's a farmer . . . plenty.** He had hoped to sell at a high price if there was a scarcity. See Introduction, p. 9.

8–9. **here's an equivocator . . .** Perhaps an allusion to the trial of Henry Garnet (see Introduction, p. 9). It is, however, impossible to say how definite the reference really is. The idea of the wickedness of 'dissimulation' and 'equivocation' was very much in the air, and was associated in the public mind with the Jesuits, whose principles were sufficiently illustrated by the plots to murder Queen Elizabeth and the Gunpowder Plot of 1605. The Jesuits were thought to hold in an extreme form the Machiavellian doctrine that the end justifies the means.

14. **French hose.** The fashion of ample French hose tempted the dishonest tailor of the time to order an excessive quantity of cloth of which he kept some for himself.

19. **the primrose way :** because 'broad is the way, that leadeth to destruction'. Cf. also 'facilis descensus Averni'.

23. **the second cock.** Cf. *Romeo and Juliet*:

> the second cock hath crow'd,
> The curfew-bell hath rung, 'tis three o'clock. (IV. iv. 3–4.)

46–7. **[tongue nor heart . . . conceive nor name:** chiasmic order.]

50. **The Lord's anointed temple.** 'A blending of two Scriptural phrases: "the Lord's anointed" (as in *Richard III*, IV. iv. 151) and "Ye are the temple of the living God"' (C. H. Herford). For the first phrase, see 1 Sam. xxvi. 9; for the second, 2 Corinthians, vi. 16.

63. **Ring the bell.** Sir E. K. Chambers says that these words are a note to the prompter that got into the text. In that case, 'What's the business' completes the half-line 'To countenance this horror!'

70–1. **Woe, alas! . . . house?** A. C. Bradley calls these words 'a mistake in acting'. The rest of his comment is a useful warning to those who are inclined to exaggerate the evidence for Lady Macbeth's humanity (see note on I. vii. 54–5; II. ii. 13–14): 'This mistake . . . shows that she does not even know what the natural feeling in such circumstances would be; and Banquo's curt answer, "Too cruel any where", is almost a reproof of her insensibility.'

74–9. 'This is no mere acting. The language here has none of the false rhetoric of his merely hypocritical speeches. It is meant to deceive, but it utters at the same time his profoundest feeling' (A. C. Bradley). Contrast ll. 94–9.

94–9. These lines are a piece of deliberate rhetoric. Macbeth is assuming a passion which he does not feel, and the only effect which he can convey into his language is one of violence. 'Silver skin' and 'golden blood' are both unnatural phrases: they are meant to jar on the mind and to indicate that Macbeth's emotion is hypocritical.

101. **Help me hence, ho!** Rowe's stage-direction at this point in his edition of Shakespeare (1709) is 'Seeming to faint'. For a discussion whether Lady Macbeth's swoon is real or assumed, see Bradley, *Shakespearean Tragedy*, pp 484–6.

106. An auger is a carpenter's tool for boring holes in wood. Donalbain feels that treachery is lurking everywhere, and his fate may be ambushed in some minute spot which is barely visible. The

metaphor was probably suggested by the words in Scot's first chapter, 'They can go in and out at auger-holes' (A. C. Bradley). Reginald Scot was the author of *The Discouerie of Witchcraft* (1584).

125-6. 'Near' is etymologically the comparative of 'nigh', and is used in that sense here. The phrase is analogous to 'the more, the merrier'. Duncan was Macbeth's first cousin. Donalbain means 'we cannot trust Macbeth's smiles: the nearer he is to us in blood, the more likely he is to prove bloodthirsty'.

ACT II. Scene IV

The first half of this scene fulfils the part of background to a picture: we see the frenzied heavens repeating the horrors of the human world. The second half briefly indicates the measure of success which has attended Macbeth since his crime: the grooms are held to have killed Duncan at the instigation of the king's sons, whose flight has involved them in suspicion; Macbeth is mounting the steps of the throne. On the other hand, Macduff—a man of great note in the realm—has conceived suspicions of his own, and refuses to attend the new king's investiture.

The signs and omens in this scene are borrowed by Shakespeare from Holinshed's Duff-Donwald story. (See Introduction pp. 11–12)

27-9. Thoughts on the enormity of violating the instincts of nature are constantly recurring in *King Lear*, a play probably written just before *Macbeth*. Cf. *King Lear*, IV. ii. 46–50:

> If that the heavens do not their visible spirits
> Send quickly down to tame these vile offences,
> It will come,
> Humanity must perforce prey on itself,
> Like monsters of the deep.

31. **Scone**: the ancient royal city of Scotland. It lay two miles north of the present town of Perth.

33. **Colmekill** (i.e. St. Columba's *cell*) is another name for Iona, one of the Western Isles of Scotland. It was the burial-place of the ancient Scottish kings.

ACT III. Scene I

Macbeth is king, but in Banquo he sees an obstacle to his happiness and security. If Banquo with Fleance, his son, can be destroyed, then, he thinks, the promise of the Witches to Banquo, 'Thou shalt get kings, though thou be none' may, perhaps, be falsified. With cold-blooded deliberation, he elicits from Banquo the necessary information as to his movements, and commits the task of murdering him to two professional cut-throats. Evidently he is now so blind as to believe that a crime performed by deputy will not be visited on the principal (cf. III. iv. 50).

8–10. 'Why may not the Witches, in virtue of their prophecies about you which have been proved true, turn out to be oracles for me also, and establish my hopes?'

13. **all-thing:** cf. the adverbial use of 'nothing' in a phrase like 'nothing loth'.

19, 24, and 36. The apparently casual way in which Macbeth slips in three necessary questions shows how far he has improved in cold-blooded efficiency since the murder of Duncan.

23. **we'll take to-morrow:** i.e. for our council, or for receiving your advice. If we were to read 'take 't' (it) to-morrow' the construction would be easier still. The word 'to-morrow' is repeated in l. 33: Macbeth loses no opportunity of allaying any suspicions which Banquo may have.

28–9. Another instance of Dramatic Irony.

44. **God be with you:** scan 'good-bye'.

55–7. Cf. *Antony and Cleopatra*, II. iii. 18–22:

> O Antony! stay not by his side;
> Thy demon—that's thy spirit which keeps thee,—is
> Noble, courageous, high, unmatchable,
> Where Caesar's is not; but near him thy angel
> Becomes a fear, as being o'erpower'd.

Here 'angel' and 'demon' are both varieties of 'genius', the guardian spirit who gradually becomes identified with a man's own character.

63. **unlineal.** The form of this word, and 'fruitless' and 'barren' are explained by the next half-line. All usurpers desire to found a line.

64–70. These lines have the accent of genuine feeling. Though his scruples are partly superstitious, Macbeth is not yet dead to eternal issues. His boast to 'jump the life to come' (I. vii. 7) was spoken only with the lips, not from the heart.

81. [See Note at the end of Appendix III.]

105. **takes your enemy off.** See note on I. v. 66. Macbeth continues to speak euphemistically in ll. 135–8: 'Fleance his son . . . must embrace the fate Of that dark hour.' The roundabout

language of Macbeth's directions to the Murderers is in strong
contrast to the similar scene in which King John gives orders to
Hubert for the murder of Arthur:

King John. Death.
Hubert.   My lord?
King John.   A grave.
Hubert.   He shall not live.
(*King John*, III. iii. 66.)

John has no fear of plain-speaking: Macbeth has a superstitious
dread of calling things by their right names.

116. [**distance.** The etymological meaning of the word is 'standing
apart' 'separation', and this gives the primary meaning. Its secondary
sense is an interval of space, as in fencing.]

130. [**the perfect spy o' the time.** It is a fairly common practice of
Shakespeare to substitute the passive for the active sense of a word.
Thus, in *King Lear* (IV. vi. 218), 'the main descry' means not 'what
descries' but 'what *is* descried'—'the full view of the main body'.
It is the same here. 'The perfect spy o' the time' means the *result*
of minutely inspecting or examining the time; or, as C. H. Herford
paraphrases: 'the fit moment as determined by the closest scrutiny'.
The phrase is, however, a harsh and difficult one, like many others
in *Macbeth*. Johnson proposed to read '*a* perfect spy', making Macbeth's promise refer to the Third Murderer (see Scene iii). Macbeth
is assuring the assassins that they shall not want directions to find
Banquo.]

ACT III. Scene II

A scene which indicates the changing relations between the two
chief figures of the drama. Lady Macbeth, it has been remarked,
is in some senses 'a perfect wife'. She still desires to support her
husband to the utmost, but she now sees with dreadful clearness
how empty is that 'greatness' which she had once deemed the
supreme thing in life. She has clearly no further appetite for perilous
action. Macbeth feels this, and his plans for the murder of Banquo
and Fleance are kept to himself. His own nature has changed; he
has fewer 'compunctious visitings', and any instigation from his
wife would be superfluous.

3–4. 'I seem to read relief in the answer she received, which almost
suggests that she is afraid of a further crime being committed'
(M. Leigh-Noel).

12. **what's done is done.** Notice the significant variation of this
phrase in v. i. 64–5: 'what's done cannot be undone.'

13. [**scotch'd:** Theobald's emendation for Folio 'scorch'd'.]

21–22. Than on the torture ... ecstasy. The metaphor is drawn from the torture of the rack. Here the rack on which Macbeth lies is mental torture. 'Ecstasy' indicates a frenzy or stupor caused by some overmastering passion.

23. fitful: the first known use of this word. It is one of Shakespeare's felicitous coinages.

25. Malice domestic, foreign levy: Macdonwald's rising was an example of the first, Sueno's invasion of the second.

30. [Scan *rememb(e)rance*: four syllables. The line then becomes one of the familiar type with feminine ending. See Appendix III, p. 182, and for the scansion of l. 28, see Note 1 at the end of the same.]

32–5. Perhaps a corrupt passage: 32 looks like an incomplete line. The meaning of the words as they stand is: 'We being unsafe in the meantime, seeing that we must bathe our dignities in streams of flattery towards others, and disguise our real feelings with feigned looks.' The metaphor of bathing honours in flattering streams implies that flattery has a renewing or invigorating effect on the honours.
Macbeth apologizes to his wife for asking her to be specially polite or flattering to others.

42. [**shard-born.** Some editors read 'shard-borne', i.e. borne along by shards or scaly wings.]

46. seeling. To seel (in falconry) is to close the eyes (of a hawk or other bird) by stitching up the eyelids (not the same word as 'seal').

49. bond. This may mean, alternatively, the Witches' promise to Banquo which alarms Macbeth.

51. rooky may mean 'abounding in rooks', the word being suggested by 'crow' in the preceding line; but possibly it is a dialectal word with the sense of 'misty'. The pause at the end of the incomplete line is filled by a glance from the actor towards an imaginary wood.

ACT III. SCENE III

Various theories have been offered to account for the appearance of the Third Murderer. Some editors quote III. i. 128–31, and suggest that he brings the promised instructions. The suggestion that the Third Murderer is Macbeth himself may appear attractive at first sight, but it does not bear close examination. The addition of a new figure strengthens the scene dramatically, and we need not attempt to identify him.

ACT III. Scene IV

As before, Macbeth has failed to foresee the retribution which overtakes crime; but the visitation of Banquo's Ghost is an even greater terror than the voice which cried 'Sleep no more!' Lady Macbeth rises to the occasion, and makes a desperate effort to keep up appearances before the assembled guests; but the demands on her strength are too great: she is utterly exhausted at the end of the scene, and when we see her next, it will be in the 'slumbery agitation' of her sleep-walking. On Macbeth the final effect of the banquet-scene is to complete his moral blindness and drive him to recklessness; nothing is to stand between him and 'security': 'For mine own good, All causes shall give way.'

14. **'Tis better thee without than he within.** In his momentary exultation Macbeth breaks into a grimly expressive rhyme (at the expense of grammar).

32–7. Lady Macbeth rebukes her husband for his inattention to the guests: 'My lord, you do not give friendly encouragement to the company. Any feast which is not constantly proved to be given with welcome, while it is in progress, might as well be paid for. If mere eating were the object, better remain at home. As guests, people need friendly courtesy to give a flavour to their food; without it meeting together is incomplete.'

33. To *give* or *make* cheer was a phrase meaning 'to give a friendly welcome'.

58. **Are you a man?** (said aside, like the rest of her words to l. 74). Cf. I. vii. 49–51.

72. The meaning is: we must leave corpses to be consumed by carrion birds, otherwise the dead may return.

101. **the Hyrcan tiger.** Hyrcania, south of the 'Hyrcanian' or Caspian sea, was famous for its tigers. The ultimate source of the allusion is Pliny's *Natural History*.

105. [inhabit may be either intransitive or transitive. If intransitive, the sentence means: 'If I remain or abide, trembling.' If transitive, it means: 'If I dwell in (a state of) trembling.']

124–6. **Augurs. . . .** The Folio reading is 'augures' which could formerly mean 'auguries'. 'Augury' was the practice of divining from the flight of birds. To 'understand relations' in augury is 'to know how those things relate to each other, which have no visible combination or dependence' (Johnson). Hence the meaning of ll. 124–6 is: 'Divination and the understanding of the hidden connexion of things and events, by means of magpies, jackdaws, and rooks, have brought to light murderers whose deeds were done in complete secrecy.'

133. [betimes: scan *'times*; we-ird: two syllables, as in I. iii. 32, IV. i. 136.]

ACT III. SCENE V

[The introduction of the Witches immediately after Macbeth's words in the last scene (ll. 132–3) seems natural enough, yet in some respects this scene does not appear wholly in harmony with the rest of the play, and there are critics who have doubted its authenticity. Their view is founded on the following arguments: (*a*) the appearance of the new figure of Hecate adds nothing to the impressiveness of the three Witches; (*b*) her speech is wholly lacking in the grim power of the Witches' incantations; (*c*) the style of her verse is different, for while the Witches speak in a trochaic rhythm (e.g. 'Double, double toil and trouble'), Hecate's less powerful lines are iambic (e.g. 'Upon the corner of the moon'). (See also note on ll. 11–12.) It may be urged on the other side that Hecate was a very familiar figure to an Elizabethan audience, and that a play introducing witches would seem incomplete without her. One must admit that doubts of the authenticity of the scene fall short of certainty.]

1. **Hecate**: scan as two syllables, not, as Greek requires, three.

5. Their *riddle* was the prophetic greeting which caused Macbeth to compass the death of Duncan and Banquo.

11–12. [A critic who doubts whether this scene is by Shakespeare asks pertinently: 'How, so far as the Witches are concerned, has Macbeth proved "a wayward son, spiteful and wrathful"?']

15. 'Acheron' as used here must be a poetical name to fit some gloomy spot where Hecate was wont to meet the Witches. It was really the name of the river of woe in the lower world of classical mythology, which gives it suitable associations.

20. **I am for the air.** In *The Witch* (Act III. Scene iii), a play by Shakespeare's contemporary, Thomas Middleton, Hecate says: 'I'm for aloft.' Cf. Milton's description of the Night-Hag 'riding through the air' (*Paradise Lost*, ii. 663).

23. 'Classical magic ascribed to the moon certain exudations (virus lunae) which, under the spells of the enchanter, were shed upon earthly objects' (C. H. Herford).

33. [The 'song' (which appears in full in *The Witch*, III. iii, by Middleton) begins:

Come away, come away,
Hecate, Hecate, come away!

The relation between *Macbeth* and *The Witch* has given rise to much discussion. The text of *Macbeth* in Folio contains stage-directions (III. v. 33 and IV. i. 43) for two songs from *The Witch*. *The Witch*, in its turn, contains certain verbal resemblances to *Macbeth*. The most plausible theory of the relation between the two plays is that Middleton, who wrote his play at an uncertain date before his death in 1627, took from *Macbeth* certain suggestions for *The Witch*; then, as *The Witch* enjoyed some popularity, these two songs were borrowed from it, and added to the stage-version of *Macbeth* on which the text of Folio is based.]

ACT III. Scene VI

In the highly ironical speech which opens this scene, Lennox comes forward as the spokesman of the Scottish peers. Suspicion of Macbeth's guilt now amounts to certainty. To both Lennox and the Lord, Macbeth is now the 'tyrant', and we begin to perceive the outline of the general movement which will lead to his overthrow. The Scottish leader of the rising is Macduff; it has the support of the English king, Edward the Confessor, and its purpose is to dethrone Macbeth in favour of Duncan's son, Malcolm.

8. [Lennox should have said *either* 'who can want the thought ?' *or* 'who cannot have the thought ?'. The combination of the two gives us a kind of double negative, like the colloquial 'I didn't never see him' = 'I never saw him'. Scan *monst(e)rous*. Cf. III. ii. 30.]

12–13. Lennox chooses words like 'pious' and 'delinquent' for the sake of irony, putting as it were an attitude of horrified respectability on to Macbeth.

22. **the tyrant's feast.** Henceforth 'tyrant' is the usual title for Macbeth. (See III. vi. 25, IV. iii. 12, IV. iii. 45, IV. iii. 104, IV. iii. 178, v. vi. 7, v. vii. 25, v. vii. 56.)

30. [An 'Alexandrine'; see Note 1 at the end of 'Appendix III.]

35. **Free from our feasts and banquets bloody knives.** The allusion is to the appearance of the Murderer of Banquo at Macbeth's banquet (Act III, Scene iv).

41. **The cloudy messenger turns me his back.** 'Cloudy' here means 'gloomy, sullen', as we say a man's brow is 'clouded'; cf. Shaftesbury: 'The Jews were naturally a very cloudy People.' 'Me' is an example of the 'ethical dative', which is used to imply 'that a person, other than the subject or object, has an indirect interest in the fact stated'. Cf. *Julius Caesar*: 'he plucked me ope his doublet and offered them his throat to cut' (I. ii. 268–9). Me = 'let me tell you', almost 'would you believe it ?'

ACT IV. Scene I

The last scene between Macbeth and the Witches. This time, he goes to meet them of his own accord. His demand leads to the presentment of three Apparitions, accompanied by three speeches. The Armed Head represents the head of Macbeth which is cut off by Macduff (v. vii. 82). The Bloody Child represents the birth of Macduff (v. vii. 44–45). The Child Crowned, with a tree in his hand, represents Malcolm (cf. 'the boy Malcolm', v. iii. 3), who orders each of his soldiers to 'hew him down a bough and bear 't before him' (v. iv. 5–8), and is afterwards crowned King of Scotland (v. vii. 104).

3. [The spelling of Folio and some editors is 'Harpier', which may represent the Latin *harpyia*, our 'harpy'.]

6. [**cold**: metrically equivalent to two syllables. So also 'fire' in ll. 11 and 21.]

16. blind-worm: also called a 'slow-worm', i.e. 'small harmless reptile between snakes and lizards'. The blind-worm was not known to be harmless in Shakespeare's time, just as the toad was perhaps wrongly thought poisonous (ll. 6–8).

23. maw and gulf. Gulf (= that which engulfs, or swallows up) is a metaphor for the stomach of an animal, and has therefore much the sense of 'maw'.

28. in the moon's eclipse. An eclipse was supposed to bode ill for any design which accompanied it; if the design was itself evil, an eclipse was, of course, a favourable season. Cf. Milton; *Lycidas*, 100–2:

> It was that fatal and perfidious bark,
> Built in the eclipse, and rigged with curses dark,
> That sunk so low that sacred head of thine.

43. Music and a Song, 'Black Spirits', &c. The first lines were:

> 'Black spirits and white, red spirits and gray,
> Mingle, mingle, mingle, you that mingle may!'

The whole song occurs in *The Witch*, v. ii. See note on III. v. 33.

93. Birnam: a hill in Perthshire, about twelve miles from Dunsinnan (Dunsinane).

[**Dunsinane** here; elsewhere in the play 'Dunsináne'.]

97. [Folio reads 'rebellious dead' which is quite possible if 'dead' is interpreted as Banquo. The emendation 'Rebellion's head' is Theobald's.]

s.d. Folio reads: 'A shew of eight Kings, and Banquo last, with a glasse in his hand.' This needs alteration, as Macbeth sees the eighth King bearing a glass, and Banquo coming after him (ll. 119, 123–4).

111. Banquo was the reputed ancestor of the Stuarts. The Stuart family was of Breton origin. Walter Stewart (or Stuart), who had joint command with Sir James Douglas at Bannockburn, married Marjory, daughter of Robert the Bruce. He died in 1326, leaving an only son, who as Robert II ascended the throne of Scotland in 1371. He was succeeded by Robert III and the six kings, called James. Mary, daughter of James V is omitted in the vision, as the Witches' prophecy related only to Kings.

121. That two-fold balls . . . carry. This line, like the rest of the 'show', is a compliment to James I, in whose reign *Macbeth* was written (See Introduction). James was the first monarch to rule over the United Kingdom of England (with Wales), Scotland, and Ireland.

[Henry VIII took the title of King of Ireland in 1542, though the real union with Ireland did not come for many years; James VI of Scotland became James I of Great Britain and Ireland in 1603.]

It is not clear why the 'balls' are 'two-fold' and the 'sceptres' are 'treble'. Possibly the distinction refers to the two *islands* and the three *kingdoms* united under one sovereign.

ACT IV. SCENE II

In the last scene Macbeth threatened to surprise the Castle of Macduff, and his action is swift. Lady Macduff and her son fall victims to an act of violence which is as senseless as it is wicked, for not only has Macduff himself escaped, but it is clear that such unbridled ferocity must recoil on the offender, sooner or later.

'The presence of the affectionate family before our eyes,—the timid lady's eloquent complaining to her cousin, of her husband's deserting them in danger,—the graceful prattle with her boy, in which she seeks relief from her melancholy forebodings,—and then the sudden entrance of Macbeth's murderous ruffians,—are all requisite to give that crowning horror, that consummately and violently revolting character to Macbeth's career, which Shakespeare has so evidently studied to impress upon it' (George Fletcher).

17. fits. Cf. *Coriolanus*, III. ii. 33: 'The violent fit o' the time craves it as physic.'

22. [A doubtful phrase, as Shakespeare does not elsewhere use 'move' as a noun. It may be a *verb* here, as usual — move with the sea.]

28-9. [**I am so much a fool** ... Laertes, in *Hamlet*, also calls weeping 'folly':

> I have a speech of fire, that fain would blaze,
> But that this folly douts it (i.e. puts it out).
> *Hamlet*, IV. vii. 191-2.]

36. **Poor birds** ... The boy has a precocious child's sense of logic: '*poor* birds', he means, 'are not worth snaring'.

81-2. **egg! Young fry.** The words express the murderer's scorn for a child who defies him. 'Egg' refers to his diminutive size; 'fry' is properly the young of fishes.

ACT IV. SCENE III

Both the purpose and the meaning of this scene need to be carefully studied. Its purpose, put briefly, is to give the spectator a sense of the forces gradually accumulating against Macbeth, and swelling at last into an anti-tyrant crusade. Notice the contrast between the almost hopeless tone in which the scene opens, and the note of confidence in which it ends. The substance of the scene is drawn from Holinshed. Malcolm, in England, has heard of Macbeth's desperate actions as king, and he has naturally come to anticipate some treacherous attack on his own life. Macduff's flight from his Castle and his abandonment of his wife and children are in themselves grounds for suspicion. Malcolm naturally wishes to put Macduff's loyalty to himself to the test. He adopts a plan which, though far-fetched and indirect, might be carried out by a skilful orator. He accuses himself of one vice after another, until at last all hope for Scotland seems lost, and Macduff's patriotism declares itself in a passionate outburst of despair (ll. 103–14). This is enough, and Malcolm has now only to explain away his own stratagem. Scarcely is this done, when Ross arrives with tidings of the outrage at Macduff's Castle. When the first agony of grief is spent, the news serves to seal the union between Macduff and Malcolm.

The reader who is inclined to think the first part of this scene unworthy of the rest of the play should suspend judgement until he has seen *Macbeth* acted. On the stage the whole scene can be made highly effective.

4. **Bestride.** The metaphor is drawn from the action of a soldier who stands over a fallen comrade to protect him.

21. Malcolm means that his suspicions won't alter Macduff, if the latter is trustworthy.

22. **the brightest:** Lucifer or Satan. 'Lucifer' (i.e. 'light-bringing') was traditionally the name of Satan before his fall.

24–5. **I have lost . . . doubts.** 'My hopes', i.e., of persuading you that I am really on your side, not an agent of Macbeth. 'My doubts', i.e. of Macduff's loyalty. The loss of Macduff's 'hopes' and the creation of Malcolm's 'doubts' are (says Malcolm) both due to Macduff's unaccountable desertion of his family.

29. **jealousies.** For the sense 'suspicions', cf. the Scots dialect verb 'jalouse' which means 'suspect'. Malcolm means: 'Let not my suspicions seem to affect your honour; they simply safeguard myself.'

34. [**affeer'd.** Folio has 'affear'd', but the word required has nothing to do with 'afeard', but is a legal term for 'settled', derived from late Latin afforare = fix a price.]

66–7. **Boundless intemperance . . . tyranny.** 'Intemperance (i.e. the immoderate indulgence of appetites) upsets the "golden mean" of Nature, and so tyrannizes over a man's character.'

93. [**perséverance:** the usual accentuation in Shakespeare.]

136–7. **the chance of goodness . . . quarrel:** 'the chance of goodness' means 'the chance that right may prevail'; 'our warranted quarrel' means 'our just, well-grounded quarrel'. The wish expressed is that the first may be as *certain* as the second.

138. The *unwelcome* things must refer to the faults of which Malcolm had accused himself. Macduff is perplexed by swift changes of feeling. Holinshed makes him weep.

152–5. Holinshed mentions the miraculous power of Edward the Confessor in helping 'those that were vexed with the disease commonly called the "king's evil"' (i.e. scrofula). Various later monarchs were supposed to transmit a healing power by their touch: James I and Charles I both 'touched' scrofulous persons, and Dr. Johnson who suffered from the disease, was 'touched', when a child, by Queen Anne.

153 **stamp:** 'a thing stamped with a certain impression', hence, a coin.

170. **modern ecstasy.** 'Modern' in Shakespeare means 'commonplace, everyday'; cf. *As You Like It*, II. vii. 156: 'Full of wise saws and modern instances.' For 'ecstasy', see note on III. ii. 22.

173. **or ere.** Both 'or' and 'ere' mean 'before'; the use of the two words together is emphatic. Cf. 'an if' used by Shakespeare, an = if.

196. **a fee-grief.** 'To hold in fee-simple' is 'to possess as absolute property'. Hence a 'fee-grief' is one which is peculiar to one person, a private grief.

214. **Let's make us medicine.** . . . For the idea cf. v. ii. 27.

216. **He has no children.** One of the most striking instances of Shakespeare's power of compressed language. The sentence is, however, possible to be interpreted in more than one way. Macduff may mean either (*a*) that Malcolm, being childless, cannot sympathize with his grief, or (*b*) that Macbeth has no children on whom he (Macduff) can avenge his own loss, or possibly (*c*) that if Macbeth had had children, he could not have ordered the slaughter of children. The point is fully discussed in Bradley's *Shakespearean Tragedy* (pp. 486–92).

234. [The Folio reading 'time' is just possible in the sense of 'the rhythm or measure of a piece of music'; but 'time' is a very natural printer's error for 'tune'.]

ACT V. Scene I

The collapse of Lady Macbeth is now complete. In the earlier scenes of the tragedy she appeared stronger than her husband; but they have now changed places; Lady Macbeth can only suffer, while Macbeth passes from one desperate action to another. In III. iv. 141, she had recommended sleep as the one thing needed by Macbeth, and now her own sleep is afflicted by terrible dreams. The sickness of her mind is vividly suggested by her perpetual longing for light (ll. 21–2), and her association of darkness with hell (l. 34). After this piece of breathless drama we do not see Lady Macbeth again, but there will come a report of her amid the clash of arms (v. v. 16), and again in the final scene (v. vii. 98–100).

33–4. **One; two.** She counts the strokes of the clock as on the night of Duncan's murder, which took place shortly after midnight. (See II. i. 3, II. iii. 23, note.)

35. . . . **afeard?** Lady Macbeth remembers her taunt of I. vii. 39–40.

41. **What!** . . . **ne'er be clean?** Notice the terrible contrast with II. ii. 68: 'A little water clears us of this deed.'

42–3. **you mar all with this starting:** cf. III. iv. 63.

44–5. **Go to** . . . **what you should not.** Critics disagree as to whether these words are addressed to the Gentlewoman or as an 'aside' to Lady Macbeth. The next sentence favours the former view. 'Go to' is an exclamation of reproof or impatience.

65. See note on III. ii. 12.

ACT V. SCENE II

The avenging forces begin to close in on Macbeth near those places of evil omen, Birnam Wood and Dunsinane.

4 [For this sense of 'mortified', cf. *Love's Labour's Lost*, I. i. 28: 'My loving lord, Dumaine is mortified', i.e. he has renounced 'these world's delights', l. 29].

15-16. [He cannot buckle . . . within the belt of rule. For 'Buckle within': cf. *Troilus and Cressida*, II. ii. 30: 'And buckle in a waist most fathomless.' One meaning of 'cause' is 'a movement which calls forth the efforts of its supporters' (*O.E.D.*); cf. 'the Puritan cause'. Hence, 'distemper'd cause' is equivalent to 'disorganized party'. The thought is carried on in l. 18.]

27. medicine. There is nothing un-Shakespearian in the metaphorical use of this word for a man (viz. Malcolm). Cf. *The Winter's Tale*, IV. iii. 600, where Camillo is called 'The med'cine of our house'.

30. sovereign. The word is applicable in a double sense, as referring to Malcolm, soon to be the 'sovereign' of Scotland, and as a medical term for any remedy of special potency. Cf. *1 Henry IV*, I. iii. 57-8:

> And telling me the sovereign'st thing on earth
> Was parmaceti for an inward bruise.

ACT V. SCENE III

Justice is on the side of Malcolm's forces, yet there still remains something heroic in the baited warrior. His lament over the loss of 'honour, love, obedience, troops of friends' is a vivid reminder of what Macbeth once was.

8. the English epicures. The good living in England as contrasted with the frugality of the North gave rise to the charge of self-indulgence; cf. the term 'pock-puddings' applied to the English by Scottish peasants (Scott, *Old Mortality*, XX).

9-10. The use of rhyming couplets in a blank-verse scene often marks a change in the tone of the dialogue from the dramatic to the sententious or proverbial: cf. V. vi. 7-10.

15. lily-liver'd. The liver was formerly regarded as 'the seat of love and of violent passions generally. A *white liver* is spoken of as characterizing a coward' (*O.E.D.*). Hence 'lily-liver'd' means 'cowardly, poor-spirited'. Cf. 'milk-liver'd' (*King Lear*, IV. ii. 50).

21-3. [Percy conjectured 'chair' for 'cheer', which improves the contrast with 'disseat', and Johnson conjectured 'May of life' to contrast with the yellow leaf. The changes are not justified, and Johnson's spoils the poetry. In the next line there seems no need to follow Dr. Onions in taking 'the sear' as a substantive = withered state (*Shakespeare Glossary*).]

44. [scan *per(i)lous*. 'Parlous' is an alternative form of the word. See *As You Like It*, III. ii. 46. We may doubt whether Shakespeare wrote 'stuff'd . . . stuff', but we are not justified in substituting a purely conjectural emendation.]

55. [**senna.** The reading of Folio is 'cyme', a word which does not resemble the name of any known drug. The emendation 'senna' is accepted by most editors.]

ACT V. SCENE IV

The hidden meaning in the prophecy which accompanied the Third Apparition (IV. i) is revealed in this Scene.

12. [**advantage to be given.** It is possible to extract a meaning from this phrase, but 'given' is very likely a printer's error (due to 'given' in the next line) for some such word as 'gain'd' or 'ta'en'. Johnson read 'a 'vantage (i.e. opportunity) to be gone'.]

ACT V. SCENE V

So complete is Macbeth's disillusionment that the news of his wife's death serves only to move him to a despairing summary of life's utter emptiness. Yet even now the warrior's instinct prevails, and there is something that stirs the blood in his reckless defiance of Fate.

11—13. [**my fell of hair . . . As life were in 't.** Cf. *Hamlet*, III. iv. 120, 121:

> Your bedded hair, like life in excrements,
> Starts up and stands an end.
>
> (excrement = 'that which grows out or forth').]

17–18. The meaning of 'should' in Elizabethan English is ambiguous, and two interpretations of these lines are possible. Macbeth may mean either that the queen must in any case have died some day and that *some* time the news of her death ('such a word') must have reached him, or possibly that the Queen ought to have died later, and that then the news would have arrived at a more fitting time. The former interpretation fits in better with what follows.

19–23. 'Men are always saying "to-morrow" (putting off evil to the future), yet every day turns by slow degrees into "to-morrow", and will continue to do so down to the end of time. And (looking backwards we see that) each day of the past ("all our yesterdays") has proved the last day for some who foolishly trusted to the future.'

23–8. 'How strange that this judgment on life, the despair of a man who had knowingly made mortal war on his own soul, should be frequently quoted as Shakespeare's own judgment, and should even be adduced, in serious criticism, as a proof of his pessimism' (A. C. Bradley).

24–6. Shakespeare drew from the stage some of his finest metaphors and similes; cf. *As You Like It*, II. vii. 139–66: 'All the world's a stage,' where the philosophy of Jaques resembles that here expressed, and *Richard II*, v. ii. 23–6:

> As in a theatre, the eyes of men,
> After a well-grac'd actor leaves the stage,
> Are idly bent on him that enters next,
> Thinking his prattle to be tedious . . .

ACT V. Scene VII

It is Macduff who tears away the last hope of Macbeth by unriddling the words of the Second Apparition, and it is the hand of Macduff which performs the final act of vengeance. The tragedy ends in a heroic strain, typified by Old Siward's refusal to allow a private grief any weight in an hour of public rejoicing.

29. [Re-enter Macbeth. Some editors make a new scene at this point.]

30. **play the Roman fool**, i.e. commit suicide to avoid capture. (There is no reference to any particular Roman.) Cf. *Julius Caesar*, v. iii. 89–90:

> *Titinius*: By your leave, gods: this is a Roman's part:
>   Come, Cassius' sword, and find Titinius' heart.

Cleopatra calls it 'the high Roman fashion'. Stoicism recommends suicide in adversity, but Christianity condemns it.

47. **my better part of man**: 'the finer or nobler attribute of my manhood, the better quality which I possess as a man,' i.e. courage, or manliness, as contrasted with the more feminine qualities. A similar phrase is used in *Paradise Lost*, where compassion reduces Adam to weeping:

> compassion quell'd
> His best of Man, and gave him up to tears.
>
> (*P.L.* xi. 491–4.)

50–1. i.e. What they said has been true in the literal sense of the words but untrue in its essence, in the impression they gave me.

55. **Painted upon a pole.** To suspend the picture of a 'monster' (cf. l. 54) upon a pole was a means of attracting the public to a show. The Elizabethan crowds had a great appetite for exhibited

'monsters'. Cf. *The Tempest*, II. ii. 31–3: 'There (i.e. in England) would this monster make a man (i.e. make his fortune); any strange beast there makes a man'.

63. **damn'd be him.** The grammar is no better than in III. iv. 14; but grammar is sacrificed to sound: 'damn'd be he' is much less effective.

93. Malcolm is credited with the introduction of the feudal system into Scotland.

SELECT LITERARY CRITICISM

'Macbeth' a Play of Strong Contrasts

Macbeth (generally speaking) is done upon a stronger and more systematic principle of contrast than any other of Shakespeare's plays. It moves upon the verge of an abyss, and is a constant struggle between life and death. The action is desperate and the reaction is dreadful. It is a huddling together of fierce extremes, a war of opposite natures which of them shall destroy the other. There is nothing but what has a violent end or violent beginnings. The lights and shades are laid on with a determined hand; the transitions from triumph to despair, from the height of terror to the repose of death, are sudden and startling; every passion brings in its fellow-contrary, and the thoughts pitch and jostle against each other as in the dark. The whole play is an unruly chaos of strange and forbidden things, where the ground rocks under our feet. Shakespeare's genius here took its full swing, and trod upon the farthest bounds of nature and passion. This circumstance will account for the abruptness and violent antitheses of the style, the throes and labour which run through the expression, and from defects will turn them into beauties. 'So fair and foul a day I have not seen', etc. 'Such welcome and unwelcome news together.' 'Men's lives are like the flowers in their caps, dying or ere they sicken.' 'Look like the innocent flower, but be the serpent under it.' The scene before the castle-gate follows the appearance of the Witches on the heath, and is followed by a midnight murder. Duncan is cut off betimes by treason leagued with witchcraft, and Macduff is ripped untimely from his mother's womb to avenge his death. Macbeth after the death of Banquo, wishes for his presence in extravagant terms, 'To him and all we thirst', and when his ghost appears, cries out, 'Avaunt and quit my sight', and being gone, he is 'himself again'. Macbeth resolves to get rid of Macduff, that 'he may sleep in spite of thunder'; and cheers his wife on the doubtful intelligence of Banquo's taking-off with the encouragement—'Then be thou jocund: ere the bat has flown his cloistered flight; ere to black

Hecate's summons the shard-born beetle has rung night's yawning peal, there shall be done—a deed of dreadful note.' In Lady Macbeth's speech, 'Had he not resembled my father as he slept, I had done 't', there is murder and filial piety together; and in urging him to fulfil his vengeance against the defenceless king, her thoughts spare the blood neither of infants nor old age. The description of the Witches is full of the same contradictory principle; they 'rejoice when good kings bleed', they are neither of the earth nor the air, but both; 'they should be women, but their beards forbid it'; they take all the pains possible to lead Macbeth on to the height of his ambition, only to betray him 'in deeper consequence', and after shewing him all the pomp of their art, discover their malignant delight in his disappointed hopes, by that bitter taunt, 'Why stands Macbeth thus amazedly?' We might multiply such instances everywhere.

From HAZLITT: *Characters of Shakespeare's Plays* (1817).

Of all Shakespeare's plays *Macbeth* is the most rapid, *Hamlet* the slowest in movement.

COLERIDGE.

The 'Veiled Confusion of Motive' in 'Macbeth'

THERE is in Macbeth the same kind of inconsistency as in Angelo. That it is less obvious is partly due to our personal remoteness from bloody ambition, and partly to its being overshadowed by the darker mysteries of the play, but partly also because of the means devised to conceal it. The interest in the tragedy of *Macbeth* is the perpetration of crime by a man whose magnificent qualities of mind, extreme courage, and poetic imagination, raise the villainies above common meanness, and give occasion for a superhuman conflict of images and ideas. Now though critics have explained that Macbeth lived in a world of material considerations, while his morality was merely imaginative (I wonder whether this divorce of his imagination from his ambition may not weaken the latter as a motive), yet the commonsense objection that such a man would not have committed such actions is strong and must be met. How, then, does Shakespeare meet it? If he had had any plain psycho-logical conception, we should expect the drama to reveal it; but his method here is not so much to reveal as to confuse. Judging from the text, he does not wish us to be clearly deter-mined as to whether Macbeth's ambition had preconceived and decided on the murder of Duncan; or whether the idea was chiefly imposed upon him by a supernatural devilry; or whether he was mainly urged to it by his wife, and was infected and led by her. We may combine the two latter motives, and see hell and home leagued against him: the difficulty lies in the un-known quantity of the first motive, his predisposition; which, if it be allowed to be only in the exact balance required for these other agencies to carry it, is still contradictory to the picture of nobility impressed on us by Shakespeare, and essential to his drama. The case may be put baldly thus: it would not be untrue to the facts as presented by Shakespeare, to precede the drama with a scene in which Macbeth and Lady Macbeth should in Machiavellian composure deliberate together upon the murder of Duncan: but plainly such a scene would destroy the drama.

Now this veiled confusion of motive is so well managed that it must be recognized as a device intended to escape observation. That the main conception of the play is magnificent is amply proved by the effects obtained; but they are none the less procured by a deception, a liberty of treatment or a 'dis-honesty', which is purposely blurred. The naturalness is merely this, that in nature we cannot weigh or know all the motives or springs of action, and therefore we are not shocked at not being able to understand Macbeth; the difficulty indeed is one main source of our pleasure, and is intended to be so: but this is not nature, in the sense of being susceptible of the same analysis as that by which the assumptions of science would investigate nature.

The interest in a Shakespearian tragedy lies chiefly in the hero's conduct, and is greater as his conduct surprises while it satisfies: and from the constitution of things it is difficult to imagine a character or personality whose actions shall be at once consistent and surprising. The extreme of virtue may surprise; but Shakespeare never chose to depict men of whom the world was not worthy. Then there is the extreme of vice;

and Shakespeare has surprised us with this in Iago and others; and he has surprised us, successfully or not, with monstrous forms of special qualities in Timon and in Coriolanus: but to sustain surprise in a worthy hero he has sometimes had recourse to devices which are intended to baulk analysis. In order to attain the surprises, he will risk, or even sacrifice, the logical and consistent; and as such a flaw, if it were perceived, must ruin the interest, he is ready with abundant means to obscure the inconsistency. It seems to me that one method was to take advantage of uncertainty or confusion in motives or matters of fact lying partly or wholly outside the drama, which, if they were clearly conceived as determined one way or another, would confine the action within lesser lines. Some matter which, as it appears to us, might have happened as well one way as another, is purposely left half-determined: we are led to suppose that it happened one way, and if we are disturbed by conduct inconsistent with that surmise, we can shift our surmise, but only to be encountered by actions which drive us back upon it, or suggest another explanation. The pleasure attending our surprise gratifies us, and our critical faculty is quieted by the reflection that there must be a solution, and that it is natural enough that we should not hit upon it at once. This attitude of mind is further assured by the convincing verisimilitude and richness of Shakespeare's detail, as well as by the appearance of necessity which accompanies the presentation of action.

From ROBERT BRIDGES, *The Influence of the Audience on Shakespeare's Drama* (1927).

Irony in 'Macbeth'

THROUGH its strong simplicity of plot, its flattening of the stage as of all the subsidiary characters, its working out of vengeance by agents who are carefully kept as mere puppets in the hand of Heaven, *Macbeth* bears a resemblance unique among Shakespeare's writings to Greek Tragedy; nor can it by accident be full of that irony in which the Greek tragedians— say Sophocles—delighted.

But it is to be observed that the irony most prevalent in

Macbeth is, if not an invention of Shakespeare's own, at least
different from the usual tragic irony, that consists in making
the protagonist utter words which, coming on the momentary
occasion to his lips, convey to the audience (who know what he
does not) a secondary, sinister, prophetic meaning.

There is, to be sure, some of this traditional tragic irony in
Macbeth: but its *peculiar* irony is retrospective rather than
prophetic. It does not prepare the spectator for what is to come;
but rather, when it comes, reminds him as by an echo that it
has been coming all the while. Thus, when Macbeth and Lady
Macbeth stare—how differently!—at their bloodied fingers,
he says

> 'Will all great Neptune's ocean wash this blood
>   Clean from my hand?'

She says confidently,

> 'A little water clears us of this deed.'

The irony is not yet. It comes in after-echo, in the sleep-
walking scene, when (*he* having passed beyond account of it)
she says, 'Here's the smell of blood still! All the perfumes of
Arabia will not sweeten this little hand.'

So when the ghost of Banquo seats itself at the feast, we
catch, as by echo, the insistent invitation,

> 'Fail not at our feast,'

with the promise,

> 'My lord, I will not':

as, when Macbeth calls out on the same ghost,

> 'What man dares, I dare:
>   Take any shape but that!'

we hear again,

> 'I dare do all that may become a man:
>   Who dares do more is none.'

Again, when Birnam Wood comes to Dunsinane, do we not
catch again the whisper,

> 'Stones have been known to move and trees to speak'?

The whole play, as it were a corridor of dark Inverness

Castle, resounds with such echoes: and I know no other tragedy
that so teems with these peculiar whispers (as I will call them)
of reminiscent irony.

From QUILLER-COUCH, *Shakespeare's Workmanship* (1918).

Irony as a Form of Action in 'Macbeth'

IN modern thought, then, Irony is Justice in a mocking humour.
The mockery that suddenly becomes apparent in the mysterious operations of Providence, and is a measure of their over-
powering force, is clearly capable of giving a highly dramatic
interest to a train of events, and so is fitted to be a form of
dramatic action. The operation of Destiny as exhibited in the
plot of *Macbeth* is throughout tinctured with irony: the element
of mockery appearing always in this, that apparent checks to
Destiny turn out the very means Destiny chooses by which to
fulfil itself. Irony of this kind is regularly attached to what
I have called the third variety of the Oracular Action, that in
which the oracle is fulfilled by the agency of attempts to oppose
it; but in the play under consideration the destiny, whether
manifesting itself in that type of the Oracular Action or not, is
never dissociated from the attitude of mockery to resistance
which converts obstacles into stepping-stones. It remains
to show how the rise of Macbeth, the fall of Macbeth, and
again the rise and fall taken together, are all of them Irony
Actions.

The basis of Macbeth's rise is the Witches' promise of the
crown. Scarcely has it been given when an obstacle starts up to
its fulfilment in the proclamation of Malcolm as heir-apparent.
I have already pointed out that it is this very proclamation
which puts an end to Macbeth's wavering, and leads him to
undertake the treasonable enterprise which only in the previous
scene he had resolved he would have nothing to do with.
Later in the history a second obstacle appears: the king is
slain, but his two sons, this heir-apparent and his brother,
escape from Macbeth's clutches and place two lives between
him and the fulfilment of his destiny. But, as events turn out,
it is this very flight of the princes that, by diverting suspicion
to them for a moment, causes Macbeth to be named as Duncan's

successor. A conversation in the play itself is devoted to making this point clear.

> *Ross.* Is 't known who did this more than bloody deed?
> *Macduff.* Those that Macbeth hath slain.
> *Ross.*   Alas, the day!
> What good could they pretend?
> *Macduff.*   They were suborn'd.
> Malcolm and Donalbain, the king's two sons,
> Are stol'n away and fled, which puts upon them
> Suspicion of the deed.
> *Ross.*   'Gainst nature still!
> Thriftless ambition, that wilt ravin up
> Thine own life's means! Then 'tis most like
> The sovereignty will fall upon Macbeth.
> *Macduff.* He is already nam'd, and gone to Scone
> To be invested.

Twice, then, in the course of the rise Destiny allows obstacles to appear only for the sake of using them as an unexpected means of fulfilment. The same mockery marks the fall of the action. The security against a fall promised by the Apparitions to Macbeth had just one drawback—'beware Macduff'; and we have already had occasion to notice Macbeth's attempt to secure himself against this drawback in the completest manner by extirpating the dangerous thane and his family to the last scion of his stock, and also how this cruel purpose succeeded against all but Macduff himself. Now it is to be noted that this attempt against the fulfilment of the destined retribution proves the very source of the fulfilment, without which it would never have come about. For at one point of the story Macduff, the only man who, according to the degrees of Fate, can harm Macbeth, resolves to abandon his vengeance against him. In his over-cautious policy Macduff was unwilling to move without the concurrence of Malcolm the rightful heir. In one of the most singular scenes in all Shakespeare Macduff is represented as urging Malcolm to assert his rights, while Malcolm (in reality driven by the general panic to suspect even Macduff) discourages his attempts, and affects to be a monster of iniquity, surpassing the tyrant of Scotland himself. At last he succeeds in convincing Macduff of his villainies, and in a burst of despair the fate-appointed avenger renounces vengeance.

> *Macduff.*   Fit to govern!
> No, not to live ... Fare thee well!
> These evils thou repeat'st upon thyself
> Have banish'd me from Scotland. O my breast,
> Thy hope ends here!

Malcolm, it is true, then drops the pretence of villainy, but he does not succeed in reassuring his companion.

> *Macduff.* Such welcome and unwelcome things at once
> 'Tis hard to reconcile.

At this moment enters Ross with the news of Macbeth's expedition against Fife, and tells how all Macduff's household, 'wife, children, servants, all', have been cut off 'at one swoop': before the agony of a bereavement like this hesitation flies away for ever.

> Gentle heavens,
> Cut short all intermission; front to front
> Bring thou this fiend of Scotland and myself;
> Within my sword's length set him: if he 'scape,
> Heaven forgive him too!

The action taken by Macbeth with a view to prevent Macduff's being the instrument of retribution, is brought by a mocking Fate to impel Macduff to his task at the precise moment he had resolved to abandon it.

Finally, if the rise and the fall be contemplated together as constituting one action, this also will be found animated by the same spirit of irony. The original promise of the Witches, as well as the later promise of the Apparition, had its drawback in the destiny that Banquo was to be lesser than Macbeth and yet greater, to get kings though to be none; and to secure against this drawback is Macbeth's purpose in his plot against Banquo and Fleance, by which the rival family would be extirpated. The plot only *half succeeds*, and by its half-success contributes to the exactness with which the destiny is fulfilled. Had Macbeth's attempt fully succeeded, Banquo would neither have got kings nor been one; had no such attempt at all been made, then, for anything to the contrary in the play, Banquo would have preceded his sons on the throne, and so again the oracle would not have been fulfilled which made Banquo lesser than Macbeth. But by the mixture of success and failure in Macbeth's plot Banquo is slain before he can attain the crown, and Fleance lives to give a royal house to Scotland. Once more, then, mockery appears a characteristic of the Destiny that finds in human resistance just the one peculiar device needed for effecting the peculiar distribution of fortune it has promised.

Such is the subtlety with which Shakespeare has constructed this plot of *Macbeth*, and interwoven in it Nemesis and Destiny. To outward appearance it is connected with the rise and fall of a sinner: the analysis that searches for inner principles of construction traces through its incidents three forms of action working harmoniously together, by which the rise and fall of Macbeth are so linked as to exhibit at once a crime with its Nemesis, an Oracle with its fulfilment, and the Irony which works by the agency of that which resists it. Again the separate halves of the play, the rise and the fall of the hero, are found to present each the same triple pattern as the whole. Once more, with the career of Macbeth are associated the careers of Banquo and Macduff, and these also reflect the threefold spirit. Macbeth's rise involves Banquo's fall: this fall is the subject of oracular prediction, it is the starting-point of nemesis on Macbeth, and it has an element of irony in the fact that Banquo *all but* escaped. With Macbeth's fall is bound up Macduff's rise; this also had been predicted in oracles, it is an agency in the main nemesis, and Macduff's fate has the irony that he *all but* perished at the outset of his mission. Through all the separate interests of this elaborate plot, the three forms of action— Nemesis, the Oracular, Irony—are seen perfectly harmonised and perfectly complete. And over all this is thrown the supernatural interest of the Witches, who are agents of nemesis working by the means of ironical oracles.

From MOULTON, Shakespeare as a Dramatic Artist (1885).

On the Knocking at the Gate in 'Macbeth'

FROM my boyish days I had always felt a great perplexity on one point in *Macbeth*. It was this: the knocking at the gate, which succeeds to the murder of Duncan, produced to my feelings an effect for which I never could account. The effect was, that it reflected back upon the murder a peculiar awfulness and a depth of solemnity; yet, however obstinately I endeavoured with my understanding to comprehend this, for many years I never could see *why* it should produce such an effect.

In *Macbeth*, for the sake of gratifying his own enormous and teeming faculty of creation, Shakespeare has introduced two murderers: and, as usual in his hands, they are remarkably discriminated: but, though in Macbeth the strife of mind is greater than in his wife, the tiger spirit not so awake, and his feelings caught chiefly by contagion from her,—yet, as both were finally involved in the guilt of murder, the murderous mind of necessity is finally to be presumed in both. This was to be expressed; and on its own account, as well as to make it a more proportionable antagonist to the unoffending nature of their victim, 'the gracious Duncan', and adequately to expound 'the deep damnation of his taking off', this was to be expressed with peculiar energy. We were to be made to feel that the human nature, i.e. the divine nature of love and mercy, spread through the hearts of all creatures, and seldom utterly withdrawn from man—was gone, vanished, extinct; and that the fiendish nature had taken its place. And, as this effect is marvellously accomplished in the *dialogues* and *soliloquies* themselves, so it is finally consummated by the expedient under consideration; and it is to this that I now solicit the reader's attention. If the reader has ever witnessed a wife, daughter, or sister in a fainting fit, he may chance to have observed that the most affecting moment in such a spectacle is *that* in which a sigh and a stirring announce the recommencement of suspended life. Or, if the reader has ever been present in a vast metropolis, on the day when some great national idol was carried in funeral pomp to his grave, and, chancing to walk near the course through which it passed, has felt powerfully in the silence and desertion of the streets, and in the stagnation of ordinary business, the deep interest which at that moment was possessing the heart of man—if all at once he should hear the death-like stillness broken up by the sound of wheels rattling away from the scene, and making known that the transitory vision was dissolved, he will be aware that at no moment was his sense of the complete suspension and pause in ordinary human concerns so full and affecting, as at that moment when the suspension ceases, and the goings-on of human life are suddenly resumed. All action in any direction is best expounded, measured, and made apprehensible, by reaction. Now apply this to the case in *Macbeth*. Here, as I have said, the retiring of the human heart, and the entrance of the fiendish heart was to be expressed and made sensible. Another world has stept in; and the murderers are taken out of the region of human things, human purposes, human desires. They are transfigured: Lady Macbeth is 'unsexed'; Macbeth has forgot that he was born of woman; both are conformed to the image of devils; and the world of devils is suddenly revealed. But how shall this be conveyed and made palpable? In order that a new world may step in, this world must for a time disappear. The murderers, and the murder must be insulated—cut off by an immeasurable gulf from the ordinary tide and succession of human affairs—locked up and sequestered in some deep recess; we must be made sensible that the world of ordinary life is suddenly arrested—laid asleep—tranced—racked into a dread armistice; time must be annihilated; relation to things without abolished; and all must pass self-withdrawn into a deep syncope and suspension of earthly passion. Hence it is, that when the deed is done, when the work of darkness is perfect, then the world of darkness passes away like a pageantry in the clouds: the knocking at the gate is heard; and it makes known audibly that the reaction has commenced; the human has made its reflux upon the fiendish; the pulses of life are beginning to beat again; and the re-establishment of the goings-on of the world in which we live first makes us profoundly sensible of the awful parenthesis that has suspended them.

From DE QUINCEY, *On the Knocking at the Gate in 'Macbeth'* (1823).

The Character of Macbeth

THERE is in Macbeth one marked peculiarity, the true apprehension of which is the key to Shakespeare's conception. This

bold ambitious man of action has, within certain limits, the
imagination of a poet,—an imagination on the one hand
extremely sensitive to impressions of a certain kind, and,
on the other, productive of violent disturbance both of mind
and body. Through it he is kept in contact with supernatural
impressions and is liable to supernatural fears. And through
it, especially, come to him the intimations of conscience and
honour. Macbeth's better nature—to put the matter for clearness' sake too broadly—instead of speaking to him in the overt
language of moral ideas, commands, and prohibitions, incor-
porates itself in images which alarm and horrify. His imagination is thus the best of him, something usually deeper and
higher than his conscious thoughts; and if he had obeyed it
he would have been safe. But his wife quite misunderstands
it, and he himself understands it only in part. The terrifying
images which deter him from crime and follow its commission,
and which are really the protest of his deepest self, seem to his
wife the creations of mere nervous fear, and are sometimes
referred by himself to the dread of vengeance or the restless-
ness of insecurity. His conscious or reflective mind, that is,
moves chiefly among considerations of outward success and
failure, while his inner being is convulsed by conscience.
And his inability to understand himself is repeated and exaggerated in the interpretations of actors and critics, who represent him as a coward, cold-blooded, calculating, and pitiless,
who shrinks from crime simply because it is dangerous, and
suffers afterwards simply because he is not safe. In reality his
courage is frightful. He strides from crime to crime, though his
soul never ceases to bar his advance with shapes of terror, or
to clamour in his ears that he is murdering his peace and cast-
ing away his 'eternal jewel'.

From BRADLEY, *Shakespearean Tragedy* (1904).

The Character of Lady Macbeth

IN the opening Act at least, Lady Macbeth is the most com-
manding and perhaps the most awe-inspiring figure that
Shakespeare drew. Sharing, as we have seen, certain traits with
her husband, she is at once clearly distinguished from him by

an inflexibility of will, which appears to hold imagination, feeling, and conscience completely in check. To her the prophecy of things that will be becomes instantaneously the determination that they shall be:

> Glamis thou art, and Cawdor; and shalt be
> What thou art promised.

She knows her husband's weakness, how he scruples 'to catch the nearest way' to the object he desires; and she sets herself without a trace of doubt or conflict to counteract this weakness. To her there is no separation between will and deed; and, as the deed falls in part to her, she is sure it will be done:

> The raven himself is hoarse
> That croaks the fatal entrance of Duncan
> Under my battlements.

On the moment of Macbeth's rejoining her, after braving infinite dangers and winning infinite praise, without a syllable on these subjects or a word of affection, she goes straight to her purpose and permits him to speak of nothing else. She takes the superior position and assumes the direction of affairs,—appears to assume it even more than she really can, that she may spur him on. She animates him by picturing the deed as heroic, 'this night's *great* business,' or 'our *great* quell,' while she ignores its cruelty and faithlessness. She bears down his faint resistance by presenting him with a prepared scheme which may remove from him the terror and danger of deliberation. She rouses him with a taunt no man can bear, and least of all a soldier,—the word 'coward'. She appeals even to his love for her:

> From this time
> Such I account thy love;

—such that is, as the protestations of a drunkard. Her reasonings are mere sophisms; they could persuade no man. It is not by them, it is by personal appeals, through the admiration she extorts from him, and through sheer force of will, that she impels him to the deed. Her eyes are fixed upon the crown and the means to it; she does not attend to the consequences. Her plan of laying the guilt upon the chamberlains is invented on the spur of the moment, and simply to satisfy her husband.

Her true mind is heard in the ringing cry with which she answers his question, 'Will it not be received . . . that they have done it?'

> Who *dares* receive it other?

And this is repeated in the sleep-walking scene: 'What need we fear who knows it, when none can call our power to account?' Her passionate courage sweeps him off his feet. His decision is taken in a moment of enthusiasm:

> Bring forth men-children only:
> For thy undaunted mettle should compose
> Nothing but males.

And even when passion has quite died away her will remains supreme. In presence of overwhelming horror and danger, in the murder scene and the banquet scene, her self-control is perfect. When the truth of what she has done dawns on her, no word of complaint, scarcely a word of her own suffering, not a single word of her own as apart from his, escapes her when others are by. She helps him, but never asks his help. She leans on nothing but herself. And from the beginning to the end—though she makes once or twice a slip in acting her part— her will never fails her. Its grasp upon her nature may destroy her, but it is never relaxed. We are sure that she never betrayed her husband or herself by a word or even a look, save in sleep. However appalling she may be, she is sublime.

From BRADLEY, *Shakespearean Tragedy* (1904).

The Capacity for Good in Macbeth and Lady Macbeth

Macbeth is not the greatest of Shakespeare's tragedies. It is neither so pitiful as *Othello* nor so awe-inspiring as *Lear*; but it is by its comparative simplicity one of the most impressive and instructive. In none is it so easy to discern the relation between our moral and our dramatic or artistic sympathies and judgements, to realize how the moral point of view is not superseded by the dramatic but absorbed and transcended. Judged from the moral point of view, as our reason compels us to judge him, a point of view from which Macbeth never is able to emancipate himself, like Iago or

Richard III, judged from the point of view of members of a society which is seeking a common good, Macbeth is condemned; we contemplate his fate with a moral approval which we certainly do *not* feel in the case of Othello or Lear. Now moral approval and disapproval is a factor, an element, in the pleasure we derive from tragedy. If with some modern novelists we supersede the will altogether, if we represent our hero as being and feeling himself to be a puppet in the hands of Fate, we weaken the tragic effect. The last drop of bitterness in the cup of the tragic hero is to realize that his own folly or guilt has brought about his destruction . . . 'then all strikes deadly inward and suffocateth'.

From both the points of view from which we contemplate a tragic event, the moral culpability, the 'error' of the hero counts for much. In as far as we identify ourselves by sympathy with the hero, as in all good tragedy we do and must, our suffering, our pity and fear, is heightened. And on the other hand, in so far as we look on him from without, as spectators, but as spectators interested in that moral law, that common good with which he is, to a greater or less degree, in conflict, the consideration of guilt determines our greater or less approval of the fate that overtakes him, the satisfaction of our sense of justice. Now in some cases the latter point of view obscures the first altogether, insomuch that Aristotle pronounces the overthrow of a bad man to be no tragedy at all. And in some Elizabethan tragedies, influenced by the Senecan conception of tragedy as a picture of a crime and the Nemesis which overtakes it, our sympathies are so alienated from the hero of the tragedy that his destruction appeals to little more than our approval of the justice of his fate. But the imagination of a great poet transcends such limitations. We recognize the guilt of Macbeth, the radical error of his will, but we recognize also how frail a thing the human will is, beset by passion and temptation and illusion. We see evil born of the very capacity for good. There is something in Macbeth and Lady Macbeth, even in their errors, that bespeaks greatness of soul more clearly than the humdrum, half-timid honesty of Banquo, or the narrow and hard virtue of Macduff; and bespeaks not only strength but fineness of soul. Macbeth is a

criminal, Bunyan a saint—but they are men of the same
imaginative temperament, the same moral susceptibilities.
And Lady Macbeth too—the courage which carries her through
the night of the crime, the sensibility which betrays in the
sleep-walking scene how sorely it has been outraged, are of a
kind that lie outside the range of many who keep the beaten
and safer track. And so our judgements of moral approval and
disapproval are absorbed in and transcended by a sense of the
beauty and the mystery of these great human souls, their
conflict, and their defeat ; the beauty and the mystery of human
life.

H. J. C. GRIERSON (from an edition of Macbeth, 1914).

The Witches

THE Weird Sisters are as true a creation of Shakespeare's
as his Ariel and Caliban,—fates, furies, and materializing
witches being the elements. They are wholly different from
any representation of witches in the contemporary writers, and
yet presented a sufficient external resemblance to the creatures
of vulgar prejudice to act immediately on the audience.
Their character consists in the imaginative disconnected from
the good ; they are the shadowy obscure and fearfully anoma-
lous of physical nature, the lawless of human nature,—elemental avengers without sex or kin :

> Fair is foul, and foul is fair:
> Hover thro' the fog and filthy air. . . .

The true reason for the first appearance of the Witches is to
strike the key-note of the character of the whole drama, as is
proved by their reappearance in the third scene, after such an
order of the king's as establishes their supernatural power of
information.   I say information,—for so it only is as to Glamis
and Cawdor: the 'king hereafter' was still contingent,—still
in Macbeth's moral will; although, if he should yield to the
temptation, and thus forfeit his free agency, the link of cause
and effect *more physico* would then commence. I need not say,
that the general idea is all that can be required from the poet,—
not a scholastic logical consistency in all the parts so as to meet
metaphysical objectors. But O! how truly Shakespearian is the

opening of Macbeth's character given in the unpossessedness of Banquo's mind, wholly present to the present object,—an unsullied, unscarified mirror! And how strictly true to nature it is, that Banquo, and not Macbeth himself, directs our notice to the effect produced on Macbeth's mind, rendered temptible by previous dalliance of the fancy with ambitious thoughts:

> Good Sir, why do you start; and seem to fear
> Things that do sound so fair?

And then, again, still unintroitive, addresses the Witches:—

> I' the name of truth,
> Are ye fantastical, or that indeed
> Which outwardly ye show?

Banquo's questions are those of natural curiosity,—such as a girl would put after hearing a gipsy tell her schoolfellow's fortune;—all perfectly general, or rather planless. But Macbeth, lost in thought, raises himself to speech only by the Witches being about to depart:—

> Stay, you imperfect speakers, tell me more:—

and all that follows is reasoning on a problem already discussed in his mind,—on a hope which he welcomes, and the doubts concerning the attainment of which he wishes to have cleared up. Compare his eagerness,—the keen eye with which he has pursued the Witches' evanishing—

> Speak, I charge you!

with the easily satisfied mind of the self-uninterested Banquo:—

> The earth hath bubbles, as the water has,
> And these are of them. Whither are they vanish'd?

and then Macbeth's earnest reply,—

> Into the air; and what seem'd corporal melted
> As breath into the wind. *Would they had stay'd.*

Is it too minute to notice the appropriateness of the simile 'as breath' etc., in a cold climate?

Still again Banquo goes on wondering like any common spectator:

> Were such things here as we do speak about?

4123·7   F

whilst Macbeth persists in recurring to the self-concerning:—

> Your children shall be kings.
>
> *Banquo.*   You shall be king.
>
> *Macbeth.* And thane of Cawdor too: went it not so?

So surely is the guilt in its germ anterior to the supposed cause, and immediate temptation! Before he can cool, the confirmation of the tempting half of the prophecy arrives, and the concatenating tendency of the imagination is fostered by the sudden coincidence:—

> Glamis, and thane of Cawdor!
> The greatest is behind.

Oppose this to Banquo's simple surprise:—

> What, can the devil speak true?

Ib. Banquo's speech:—

> That, trusted home,
> Might yet enkindle you unto the crown,
> Besides the thane of Cawdor. . . .

Macbeth no longer hears any thing *ab extra*:—

> Two truths are told,
> As happy prologues to the swelling act
> Of the imperial theme.

Then in the necessity of recollecting himself—

> I thank you, gentlemen.

Then he relapses into himself again, and every word of his soliloquy shows the early birth-date of his guilt. He is all-powerful without strength; he wishes the end, but is irresolute as to the means; conscience distinctly warns him, and he lulls it imperfectly:—

> If chance will have me king, why, chance may crown me,
> Without my stir.

Lost in the prospective of his guilt, he turns round alarmed lest others may suspect what is passing in his own mind, and instantly vents the lie of ambition:—

> My dull brain was wrought
> With things *forgotten:*—

And immediately after pours forth the promising courtesies of a usurper in intention:—

> Kind gentlemen, your pains
> Are register'd where every day I turn
> The leaf to read them.

From COLERIDGE, *Lectures on Shakespeare* (1811–12).

I HOLD that it is incredible Shakespeare should have taken up witches into his tragedy and left them as James I and the rest of the world commonly conceived them. His imagination was far too intense, his representing power much too exacting, to allow him to leave them unidealised. It is true he kept their vulgar elements for the sake of the common folk who did not think: but for those who did, Shakespeare unvulgarised the witches.

They materialise themselves only for their purpose of temptation; their normal existence is impalpable, invisible, unearthly. When they vanish Banquo cries

> The earth hath bubbles, as the water has,
> And these are of them. Whither are they vanish'd?
> *Macbeth.* Into the air; and what seem'd corporal melted
> As breath into the wind.

Elemental beings! inhabiting the world of nature beyond our senses, from whose evil will the limits of our perception defend us. Here Shakespeare has made them, on one side of their being, the comrades or impellers of the destroying forces of nature. They meet in thunder, lightning, and in rain. They make storms; they preside over the hurly-burly of the battle. 'I conjure you', cries Macbeth, giving them, as the Norsemen to their witches, all power over destructive tempest,

> I conjure you, by that which you profess,—
> Howe'er you come to know it,—answer me;
> Though you untie the winds and let them fight
> Against the churches; though the yesty waves
> Confound and swallow navigation up;
> Though bladed corn be lodg'd and trees blown down;
> Though castles topple on their warders' heads;
> Though palaces and pyramids do slope

> Their heads to their foundations; though the treasure
> Of Nature's germens tumble all together,
> *Even till destruction sicken*; answer me
> To what I ask you.

These are their works and ways in nature, in dreadful gaiety of destruction.

But the witches are much more than creatures who have power over nature. They have influence also on the soul, but only on the soul that has admitted evil to dwell in it. When the soil is tainted their poisonous seeds take root. When a man has already sheltered a temptation they come to him charged with fresh temptation, and hurry the already cherished evil into outward execution of it. They master the thoughts of Macbeth because they are in tune with them. They have no influence on Banquo, who is innocent of wrong. Nowhere in Shakespeare is a more subtle delineation of the effect of suggested evil on two souls, one in sympathy with evil, the other not, than there is in the scene between Macbeth and Banquo after the disappearance of the witches.

From STOPFORD BROOKE, *On Ten Plays of Shakespeare* (1919).

Imagery in Macbeth

THE imagery in *Macbeth* appears to me to be more rich and varied, more highly imaginative, more unapproachable by any other writer, than that of any other single play. It is particularly so, I think, in the continuous use made of the simplest, humblest, everyday things, drawn from the daily life in a cottage, as a vehicle for sublime poetry. But that is beside our point here.

The ideas in the imagery are in themselves more imaginative, more subtle and complex than in other plays, and there are a greater number of them, interwoven the one with the other, recurring and repeating. There are at least four of these main ideas and many subsidiary ones.

[1] One is the picture of Macbeth himself . . .

The idea constantly recurs that Macbeth's new honours sit ill upon him, like a loose and badly fitting garment belonging to some one else. Macbeth himself first expresses it, quite early in the play, when, immediately following the first appearance of the witches and their prophecies, Ross arrives from the King and greets him as thane of Cawdor, to which Macbeth quickly replies,

> The thane of Cawdor lives: why do you dress me
> In borrow'd robes?

And a few minutes later, when he is rapt in ambitious thoughts suggested by the confirmation of two out of the three 'prophetic greetings', Banquo, watching him, murmurs,

> New honours come upon him,
> Like our strange garments, cleave not to their mould
> But with the aid of use.

After the murder, when Ross says he is going to Scone for Macbeth's coronation, Macduff uses the same simile:

> Well, may you see things well done there: adieu!
> Lest our old robes sit easier than our new!

And, at the end, when the tyrant is at bay at Dunsinane and the English troops are advancing, the Scottish lords still have this image in their minds.

Angus vividly sums up the essence of what they all have been thinking ever since Macbeth's accession to power,

> now does he feel his title
> Hang loose about him, like a giant's robe
> Upon a dwarfish thief.

This imaginative picture of a small, ignoble man encumbered and degraded by garments unsuited to him, should be put against the view emphasized by some critics (notably Coleridge and Bradley) of the likeness between Macbeth and Milton's Satan in grandeur and sublimity.

[2] Another image or idea which runs through *Macbeth* is the reverberation of sound echoing over vast regions, even into the limitless spaces beyond the confines of the world.

Macbeth himself, like Hamlet, is fully conscious of how impossible it is to 'trammel up the consequence' of his deed, and by his magnificent images of angels pleading trumpet-tongued, 'pity, like a naked, new-born babe, striding the blast,'

> Or heaven's cherubin, hors'd
> Upon the sightless couriers of the air,

who

> Shall blow the horrid deed in every eye,
> That tears shall drown the wind,

he fills our imagination with the picture of its being broadcast through great spaces with reverberating sound.

This is taken up again by Macduff, when he cries,

>   each new morn
> New widows howl, new orphans cry, new sorrows
> Strike heaven on the face, that it resounds
> As if it felt with Scotland and yell'd out
> Like syllable of dolour,

and again by Ross, when he is trying to break the terrible news of Macbeth's latest murders to Macduff—the destruction of his own wife and children—

>   I have words
> That would be howl'd out in the desert air,
> Where hearing should not latch them.

One can scarcely conceive a more vivid picture of the vastnesses of space than this, and of the overwhelming and unending nature of the consequences or reverberations of the evil deed.

[3] Another constant idea in the play arises out of the symbolism that light stands for life, virtue, goodness; and darkness for evil and death. 'Angels are bright', the witches are 'secret, black and mid-night hags', and, as Dowden says, the movement of the whole play might be summed up in the words, 'good things of day begin to droop and drowse'.

This is, of course, very obvious, but out of it develops the further thought which is assumed throughout, that the evil which is being done is so horrible that it would blast the sight to look on it, so darkness or partial blinding is necessary to carry it out.

Like so much in the play it is ironic that it should be Duncan who first starts this simile, the idea of which turns into a leading motive in the tragedy. When he is conferring the new honour on his son, he is careful to say that others, kinsmen and thanes, will also be rewarded:

> *Signs of nobleness, like stars, shall shine*
> On all deservers.

No sooner has the king spoken than Macbeth realizes that
Malcolm, now a Prince of the realm, is an added obstacle in his
path, and suddenly, shrinking from the blazing horror of
the murderous thought which follows, he cries to himself,

> Stars, hide your fires!
> Let not light see my black and deep desires.

And from now on, the idea that only in darkness can such evil
deeds be done is ever present with both Macbeth and his wife,
as is seen in their two different and most characteristic invoca-
tions to darkness; her blood-curdling cry

> Come thick night,
> And pall thee in the dunnest smoke of hell,

which takes added force when we hear later the poignant words,
'She has light by her continually'; and his more gentle appeal
in the language of falconry,

> Come, seeling night,
> Scarf up the tender eye of pitiful day.

And when Banquo, sleepless, uneasy, with heart heavy as lead,
crosses the courtyard on the fateful night, with Fleance
holding the flaring torch before him, and, looking up to the
dark sky, mutters,

> There's husbandry in heaven,
> Their candles are all out,

we know the scene is set for treachery and murder.

So it is fitting that on the day following 'dark night strangles
the travelling lamp', and

> darkness does the face of earth entomb
> When living light should kiss it.

The idea of deeds which are too terrible for human eyes to look
on is also constant; Lady Macbeth scoffs it, 'the sleeping and
the dead', she argues, 'are but as pictures':

> 'tis the eye of childhood
> That fears a painted devil;

but Macduff, having seen the slain king, rushes out, and cries
to Lennox,

> Approach the chamber, and destroy your sight
> With a new Gorgon.

Macbeth boldly asserts he dare look on that 'which might appal the devil', and the horror and fear he feels on seeing one 'too like the spirit of Banquo' in the procession of kings is expressed in his agonized cry,

> Thy crown does sear mine eye-balls;

while in his bitter and beautiful words at the close, the dominant thoughts and images are the quenching of light and the empty reverberation of sound and fury, 'signifying nothing'.

[4] The fourth of the chief symbolic ideas in the play is one which is very constant with Shakespeare and is to be found all through his work, that sin is a disease—Scotland is sick.

So Macbeth, while repudiating physic for himself, turns to the doctor and says if he could by analysis find Scotland's disease

> And purge it to a sound and pristine health,
> I would applaud thee to the very echo,
> That should applaud again . . .
> What rhubarb, senna, or what purgative drug,
> Would scour these English hence?

Malcolm speaks of his country as weeping, bleeding, and wounded, and later urges Macduff to

> make us medicines of our great revenge,
> To cure this deadly grief,

while Caithness calls Malcolm himself the 'medicine of the sickly weal', 'the country's purge'.

It is worth noting that all Macbeth's images of sickness are remedial or soothing in character; balm for a sore, sleep after fever, a purge, physic for pain, a 'sweet oblivious antidote', thus intensifying to the reader or audience his passionate and constant longing for well-being, rest, and, above all, peace of mind.

From C. F. E. SPURGEON, *Shakespeare's Imagery* (1935).

APPENDIX I

THE LIFE OF WILLIAM SHAKESPEARE

(condensed from Sir Edmund Chambers's *William Shakespeare*)

WILLIAM SHAKESPEARE was born of middle-class parents at
Stratford-on-Avon, a provincial market town of some importance, at an uncertain date between April 24, 1563, and April 23,
1564. His parents were natives of Warwickshire. His father,
John Shakespeare, whose principal business was that of glover,
rose high in civic life, becoming alderman in 1565 and bailiff in
1568, but later fell on evil days. His mother was Mary Arden.
Shakespeare was educated at King Edward VI's Grammar
School, Stratford, where he must have learnt a fair amount of
Latin, if little or no Greek. He married in 1582 Anne Hathaway,
and his first child, Susanna, was baptized in May 1583, to be
followed in February 1585 by twins, Hamnet and Judith.
Susanna's daughter, Elizabeth (died 1670), was the poet's last
direct descendant.

We have no certain information as to Shakespeare's life
between 1584 and 1592. There is an early tradition that he
stole deer from Sir T. Lucy of Charlecote. We know Shakespeare
was in London by 1592 but not when he went there. During
these years Shakespeare must have acquired the varied knowledge and experience of life shown in his plays.

The mention of Shakespeare in a death-bed letter of the play-
wright Greene in September 1592 shows that as a writer for
the stage Shakespeare was just becoming a serious rival to the
university wits—Marlowe, Peele, Nashe, and Lodge. The years
when the theatres were closed on account of plague gave time
for the poems *Venus and Adonis* (1593) and *Lucrece* (1594), both
dedicated to the Earl of Southampton. By March 1595 Shakespeare was a shareholder in the acting company of the Lord
Chamberlain's men, who divided with the Admiral's men the
command of the London stage from about 1594 to 1603. For
this company, which later became the King's men, Shakespeare
seems to have written during the rest of his career. After
1599 most of his plays were performed at the Globe Theatre.

Shakespeare probably wrote his *Sonnets* between 1595 and 1600, but they were not printed till 1609.

In 1596 Shakespeare obtained a grant of arms; in 1597 he bought New Place, a substantial house and garden at Stratford, but he is still found living in London in 1597, 1599, and 1604. Shakespeare occasionally appeared as an actor himself, chiefly before 1598.

About 1610 Shakespeare retired to Stratford, and he wrote no more after 1613. He took no part in civic life, and died on 23 April 1616. There is no reason to reject the report that he died of fever contracted from drinking too hard at a merry meeting with Drayton and Ben Jonson. The family is extinct.

TABLE OF APPROXIMATE DATES OF SHAKESPEARE'S PLAYS

1590–1.
  2 Henry VI.
  3 Henry VI.

1591–2.
  1 Henry VI.

1592–3.
  Richard III.
  Comedy of Errors.

1593–4.
  Titus Andronicus.
  Taming of the Shrew.

1594–5.
  Two Gentlemen of Verona.
  Love's Labour's Lost.
  Romeo and Juliet.

1595–6.
  Richard II.
  Midsummer-Night's Dream.

1596–7.
  King John.
  Merchant of Venice.

1597–8.
  1 Henry IV.
  2 Henry IV.

1598–9.
  Much Ado About Nothing.
  Henry V.

1599–1600.
  Julius Caesar.
  As You Like It.
  Twelfth Night.

1600–1.
  Hamlet.
  Merry Wives of Windsor.

1601–2.
  Troilus and Cressida.

1602–3.
   All's Well That Ends Well.

1603–4.
————

1604–5.
   Measure for Measure.
   Othello.

1605–6.
   King Lear.
   Macbeth.

1606–7.
   Antony and Cleopatra.

1607–8.
   Coriolanus.
   Timon of Athens.

1608–9.
   Pericles.

1609–10.
   Cymbeline.

1610–11.
   Winter's Tale.

1611–12.
   Tempest.

1612–13.
   Henry VIII.
   Two Noble Kinsmen.

APPENDIX II

A NOTE ON SHAKESPEARE'S LANGUAGE

By C. T. ONIONS

VOCABULARY. As the *Oxford Shakespeare Glossary* shows, there are some ten thousand words in the whole of the works attributed to Shakespeare which require explanation for the general reader, either because they are no longer in ordinary use or because they are used by him in some way that is not now familiar. Among the former are such words as *ballow* cudgel, *phill-horse* shaft-horse, and *neaf* fist, which are now only provincial, and such others as *benison* blessing, *foison* abundance, *mow* grimace, *parlous* dangerous, *puissant* powerful, *teen* grief, which may be found still in literary diction, as well as a considerable number that have been used, so far as we know, by Shakespeare alone. With such as these we become acquainted by reference to glossaries and notes. But it is possible to continue to read Shakespeare without properly understanding him because we are unaware of, and sometimes do not even suspect, differences in the meaning of words that are in general use to-day. The following selection of such words will serve to indicate the nature of the differences that may be looked for:

allow approve
argument proof, subject of discourse
brave fine, splendid
churchman clergyman
close secret
complexion habit or constitution of body or mind, look, aspect, appearance
conceit idea, thought, invention
condition covenant, rank, character
difference disagreement, dispute
evil disease
fashion sort
favour appearance, face
feature bodily form
gear affair, business
grudge complain
hint opportunity
hope expect, suppose
infer allege
instance cause, evidence, proof
level aim
lewd bad, vile

liberal unrestrained, licentious
mere absolute, downright
merely entirely
miss do without
note sign, stigma, information
obsequious dutiful
owe own
painful laborious
passion painful disease, strong emotion
peevish silly, perverse
present immediate
presently at once
prevent anticipate
quality rank, profession
rate estimation
respect consideration
sad grave, serious
shrewd mischievous, bad
sort rank, class, way, manner
still always, continually
stomach inclination, angry or proud temper
sudden swift, violent
tall fine, valiant
type mark, badge
very true, complete

Among words having a very wide range of meaning the following may be noted:

humour (1) moisture, (2) any of the four fluids of the human body recognized by the old physiologists, (3) temperament, (4) mood, temper, fancy, caprice, inclination;

nice (1) delicate, (2) shy, coy, (3) fastidious, (4) subtle,

minute, (5) trivial, (6) critical, precarious, (7) **exact,**
precise;
quaint (1) skilled, clever, (2) pretty, dainty, (3) handsome,
elegant, (4) carefully elaborated;
sensible (1) sensitive, (2) of the senses, (3) capable of emotion, (4) rational, (5) tangible, substantial, (6) full of good
sense;
wit (1) mental powers, mind, faculty of perception, as in *the
five wits*, (2) inventive power, (3) understanding, intelligence, (4) wisdom, good sense, as in *brevity is the soul of
wit*, (5) lively fancy producing brilliant talk.

A second adjective **dear** grievous, severe, dire (distinct from
dear beloved, precious) is seen in *my dear offence, thy dear exile.*
Many adjectives and participial words show the application
of a suffix with a force different from that which is now usual:

deceivable deceitful	**questionable** inviting question
tuneable tuneful	**careless** uncared for
unmeritable undeserving	**unexpressive** inexpressible
cureless incurable	**plausive** plausible
grac'd gracious	**unavoided** inevitable
guiled treacherous	**beholding** obliged, beholden
disdain'd disdainful	**timeless** untimely, premature

Note also the double meaning, active and passive, of **artificial** (1) constructive, creative, (2) produced by art.

Shakespeare uses a multitude of technical terms of the arts
and sciences; these are treated in their historical setting in
Shakespeare's England (O.U.P.); note especially the glossary of
musical terms in vol. ii, pp. 32 ff. Some general aspects of the
vocabulary are dealt with in G. S. Gordon's *Shakespeare's
English*, Society for Pure English, Tract xxix (O.U.P.).

PRONUNCIATION. In order to understand the scansion
of the verse it is necessary to bear in mind certain features of
the pronunciation of the time. Many words of French or Latin
origin had been variously stressed from early times, and devia-
tion from present usage is to be seen, for example, in Shakespeare's *adver'tizèd, aspect', canon'izèd, chas'tise, compact'*

(noun), *exile'*, *instinct'* (noun), *obdu'rate*, *reven'ue*, *sepul'chre*, *solem'nizèd*, *triumph'ing*. The stressing of certain adjectives and participles of two syllables is subject to the rule that immediately before the nouns of one syllable, and before other nouns stressed on the 1st syllable, they themselves are stressed on the 1st syllable, but in other positions on the 2nd; thus: *all' the com'plete ar'mour*, *ev'ery way' complete'*; *the en'tire sum'*, *your' entire' affec'tion*; *the crown' so foul' misplaced'*, *the mis'placed John'*.

In words in *-ian, -ience, -ient, -ion*, these endings may count as two syllables; thus, *Christian*, *patient* may be 3 syllables, *condition*, *impatience* 4, *lamentation* 5. Similarly *marriage* and *soldier* may be three syllables. There is variation in such words as *fire*, *hour*, *power*, *prayer*, which may count as either one or two syllables. *Either* and *neither* may be slurred into one syllable, and *whether* is often so reduced, the form *where* frequently occurring in the old editions, continuing what was a regular early English variant form. *Hither*, *thither*, *whither*, and *having*, *evil*, *devil* are treated in the same way. *Statue* occurs in several passages in the old editions where three syllables are required; many modern editions substitute *statua*, which was a common Tudor and Stuart form.

NOUNS. The genitive singular ending *s* may be replaced by *his*, as *the count* **his** *galleys*, *Mars* **his** *armour*. The inflexion is dropped before *sake*, e.g. *for justice sake*, *for heaven sake*. Proper names often occur without inflexion, where the genitive might be expected, or *of*: e.g. *Venice gold*, *Rome gates*, *Tiber banks*. One of the adverbial uses of the genitive is preserved in *come your ways*. Notable examples of the *n*-plural are *shoon* for *shoes*, and *eyne* (eyes), which are used chiefly for rhyme. *Aches* is of two syllables, since the noun *ache* was pronounced *aitch*, as distinct from the verb, which was regularly spelt *ake* in the old editions. Names of measures and periods of time are often uninflected, as *twelve year*, *a thousand pound*: cf. *sennight* (= seven nights) *week*.

ADJECTIVES. Adjectives are converted into nouns with greater freedom than at present: *fair* is used for beauty as well as for lady, *the general* for the public, the multitude, *the subject* for the people of a state. Note the phrases: *in few* in few words, in short; *by small and small* little by little; *the most* (= majority) *of men*. *Enow* represents the old plural of *enough*, and is so used, always following its noun or pronoun. *Mo, moe* (= more) is also plural: it represents an old comparative adverb, which was used at first with a genitive, but became in time an adjective like *more*. The plural of *other* is either *others* or *other* (e.g. *and then come in the other*).

Peculiarities in the comparison of adjectives are: the use of the suffixes where we prefer *more* and *most*, as *certainer, perfecter, violentest*; the addition of *-er* to a comparative, as *worser*; the use of *more* and *most* with comparatives and superlatives, as *more better, most best, most dearest, more worthier, most worst, most unkindest*. Note the old comparative *near*, as in *ne'er the near*. An absolute superlative may be strengthened by prefixing *one*, e.g. *one the truest-mannered*.

PRONOUNS. The distinction between the familiar or contemptuous *thou* (*thee, thy*) and the respectful *ye* (*you, your*) is in general preserved. The old weak form *a* of *he* occurs in *There was a gaming*. The commonest genitive of *it* is *his*; the present-day *its* and the obsolete *it* (as in *It had it head bit off by it young*) are about equally frequent in the old editions. Pronominal possessive forms are sometimes used as adjectives, but only in company with other possessives, as in *his and* **mine** *lov'd darling*. Note the position of the possessive in *good* **my** *liege, sweet* **my** *coz*.

There is much irregularity in the use of the cases of pronouns. *Thee* is used for *thou*, as with intransitive imperatives, *look thee, stand thee close*; also in *I would not be thee*, and the like. We find also: *between you and* I; *Is she as tall as* me*?; Which, of* he *or Adrian* . . . *?; Damn'd* be him . . . The functions of the original nominative *ye* and objective *you* are reversed in *I do beseech* ye, *if* you *bear me hard* . . .; *us* is usual for *we* in the interrogative *Shall* 's. There is no consistency in the use of *who* and *whom*; a common confusion is illustrated in *whom* they say is killed.

The relative pronouns are not discriminated according to present practice, since *which* may refer to persons and *who* to things. *The which* is very frequent; it may be used adjectivally, as in *For the which blessing I am at him upon my knees*. The nominative relative (the subject of the clause) is often absent, as in *There be some sports are painful*. After a negative or an interrogative, *but* is frequently used as a relative = that . . . not; e.g. *No man* **but** *prophesied revenge for it; What canst thou say* **but** *will perplex them more?*

VERBS. Verbs show many old forms as well as a variety of conjugation which are no longer possible in ordinary language.

Early strong forms are retained in *holp, holp'st,* alongside *helped, helped'st; spake* and *spoke* are both in use; old strong forms are replaced by weak in *becomed, shaked;* the past tenses *drunk* and *sprung* are more frequent than *drank* and *sprang;* the clipped *broke, spoke* occur beside the original participial forms *broken, spoken; catched* and *caught* are both found; many past tense forms are used for the past participle, as *eat, holp, forsook, rode, shook, swam.* Remarkable instances of the great variety of usage may be seen in *struck, strucken, stricken,* for the past participle of *strike,* and in the conjugation *write,* past tense *writ,* occasionally *wrote,* past participle *written, writ,* less frequently *wrote.* Weak verbs of which the stem ends in *d* or *t* often have shortened past participles, as *betid, heat, wed, wet.* Observe that *graft* and *hoist* are rather participles of the older verbs *graff* and *hoise* than of *graft* and *hoist.*

Present tense forms in *s* (including *is*) are not uncommonly used with plural subjects, especially where the verb precedes the subject; e.g. *What cares these roarers for the name of king?; There is no more such masters.*

There are many survivals of impersonal uses, some of them in disguise. The older forms of *I were better, Thou'rt best* were *Me were better* It would be better for me, *Thee were best* It would be best for thee; but in *You were better* the case of the pronoun became ambiguous, *you* was in time felt as a nominative, and other pronouns fell into line. The history of the development of *I am woe* (in which *woe* is felt as an adjective) from the original *Me is woe* is somewhat similar. In *Fair befall thee* the verb is impersonal and *fair* an adverb.

The uses of the subjunctive are many and various. An exceptional construction is seen in **Live** *thou* (= if thou live), *I live.* An old use of the past subjunctive is exemplified in *If you would put me to verses, Kate, why, you* **undid** (= would undo) *me.*

The infinitive of a verb of motion is often to be supplied in thought with an auxiliary verb; e.g. *I must to England; Shall we to this gear?*

ADVERBS. Adverbs, especially those of one syllable, may have the same form as their corresponding adjectives, as *dear, full, fair, near, true*; such words as *excellent, equal, instant, prodigal* are also used adverbially. When two adverbs are coupled together which would both normally have the suffix *-ly*, one of them may lack it, as in *sprightfully and bold, so lamely and unfashionable*. A rare formation is *chirurgeonly* like a surgeon. Comparative forms with the suffix are used more freely than at present; e.g. *earth*lier *happy, wise*lier.

The use of *but* in the sense of 'only' needs to be specially noticed: *but now* just now, only this moment; similarly, *but while-ere* only a short time ago, *but late* only lately. It is coupled redundantly with *only* in *He only lived but till he was a man.*

Normally, *only* should stand immediately before the words it modifies; but it is often loosely placed, as in *He only loves the world for him* (i.e. only for him).

A negative adverb (or conjunction) may be used with another negative word, superfluously from our point of view (the use was originally emphatic): *You know my father hath no child but I*, nor none *is like to have.* The negative may even be tripled: *Love no man in good earnest;* nor no *further in sport* neither. In the following a redundant negative occurs in a dependent clause after a verb of negative meaning: *You may deny that you were* not *the cause.*

PREPOSITIONS. Prepositions have many uses that differ from their present ones; for example, *for, of*, and *to* have each some ten meanings that are not current now. *Of* and *with* are both used to express the agent, as in *seen* of *us, torn to pieces* with *a bear*, or the instrument, as in *provided* of *a torch-bearer, killed* with *a thunderstroke.* With abstract nouns, *of* forms equivalents of the corresponding adjectives; e.g. *of desperation* desperate, *of nature* natural. Both *for* and *to* may be used, though in different kinds of context, = in the character of, as: e.g. *turned out of all towns and cities* for *a dangerous thing; I have a king here* to *my flatterer.* A preposition is used freely at the end of the sentence or clause, e.g. *he I am before* = he in whose presence I am; sometimes it is redundant, as in *the scene wherein we play* in; or again, it may be dropped, as in *I see thou lovest me not with the full weight that I love thee* (i.e. *with*).

At in *at door, at gate,* and the like, is descended from the earlier *atte* (two syllables), which is for *at the.*

CONJUNCTIONS. The following should be noted: *an* or *an if* if; *as* as if; *for* because; *but* if . . . not, unless; *nor . . . nor . . .* neither . . . nor . . ., *or . . . or . . .* either . . . or . . .; *or ere* before ever; *so* provided that; *that* (in much wider use than at present) for the reason that, because, in order that, so that; *whiles* while.

The full exposition of the language of Shakespeare requires a book to itself, and such will be found in E. A. Abbot's *Shakespearian Grammar* and W. Franz's *Shakespeare-Grammatik*. An illuminating sketch is Henry Bradley's essay 'Shakespeare's English' in *Shakespeare's England*, vol. ii, pp. 539–74. Selected points are treated with some fullness in *Nine Plays of Shakespeare* (O.U.P.), pp. xix–xxvi.

APPENDIX III

A NOTE ON METRE

VERSE is Shakespeare's ordinary medium, though all the plays contain a certain number of prose passages. In the tragedies prose is used for those parts which cannot be naturally subjected to the order and control of verse—in other words, for situations either below or above the normal level of emotion. The medium alike for scenes of low or rustic comedy and also for madness or delirium is therefore prose; and prose is also used for letters, and for scenes of childish prattle, either of which would seem artificial if turned into verse. According to these principles, the use of prose in *Macbeth* is not just arbitrary, but is more or less systematic. It is used in Act I, Scene v, for Macbeth's letter to his wife; in Act II, Scene iii, for the broad comedy of the Porter's speech; for that part of Act IV, Scene ii, in which Lady Macduff is conversing with her little

son; and for the scene of Lady Macbeth's sleep-walking (Act
v, Scene i).

Shakespeare's use of blank verse is a matter of the greatest
interest, and a short note cannot do it justice. The essential
points, however, will be mentioned, and the reader may explore
the subject farther for himself.

The following is an example of a *regular* or *normal* line of
blank verse:

> And sundry blessings hang about his throne
>
> (IV. iii. 158).

This line is composed of five *iambic* 'feet'. An iambic 'foot' (in
English verse) is one in which the 1st syllable is unstressed
and the 2nd stressed; for instance, the word 'away' is itself
an iambic foot. If we use ∪ for an unstressed, and / for a
stressed syllable, we may 'scan' the line as follows:

> And sun|dry bless|ings hang | about | his throne.

In this line, the 1st, 3rd, 5th, 7th, and 9th syllables are unstressed or 'weak'; the 2nd, 4th, 6th, 8th, and 10th are stressed
or 'strong'; in other words, the line consists of five iambic
feet. Another point must be made. In reading the line one's
instinct is to make a slight pause after the 5th syllable. Hence
the scansion of the line, with the pause or caesura marked, is
as follows:

> And sun|dry bless|ings || hang | about | his throne.

It is only in Shakespeare's early plays that a large proportion of the lines are as regular as the specimen quoted; a long
succession of such lines is monotonous and undramatic. As
Shakespeare became more skilful in his use of verse, he made
it increasingly responsive to the varying pressure of emotion,
thought, and feeling, the result being that his mature verse is
alive in every nerve. No one can fully describe or analyse the
secret of such verse any more than the actions of an animal
can be perfectly reproduced by a machine; the nearest approach to description is only rough-and-ready. But though
Shakespeare's verse at its best, in *Macbeth* for example, is
marvellously free, it is the reverse of chaotic. The variety is

not purchased at the expense of disorder. Shakespeare departs in an infinity of ways from the bare regularity of the five iambic feet, yet never so far as to obliterate the original pattern altogether.

A comparison between two typical passages will illustrate these points. The first is a characteristic piece of early blank verse written when poets were accustoming themselves to its 'rules' and had scarcely begun to seek the means to give it life and variety:

1. Suppóse | they bé | in núm|ber in|finíte|,
2. Yet bé|ing vóid | of márt|ial dís|ciplíne|,
3. All rún|ning héad|long gréed|y áf|ter spóils|,
4. And móre | regárd|ing gáin | than víc|tory,
5. Líke to | the crú|el bróth|ers of | the eárth|,
6. Sprúng of | the teéth | of drág|ons vén|omous|,
7. Their cáre|less swórds | shall lánce | their fél|lows' thróats|,
8. And máke | us tri|umph in | their óv|erthrów|.

(From Marlowe's *Tamburlaine*, published 1590.)

The following points are noticeable:

(*a*) The regular type of line dominates in the passage. Lines 1, 2, and 7 conform perfectly to the 'rule' of five iambic feet. The exceptions are trifling: in line 3 the stress is divided between the two syllables of the 1st foot; in line 4 the last syllable is now weak, though probably it was strong when the passage was composed; in line 5, the stress falls on the 1st syllable of the 1st foot, and there is no stress in the 4th foot; in line 6 the 1st syllable of the 1st foot is stressed, and the last syllable of the line is weak; in line 8 there is no stress in the 3rd foot.

(*b*) The sense of every line ends in itself; there are no 'overflows' of one line into another.

(*c*) The pause is always near the middle of the line (i.e. after the 4th, 5th, or 6th syllable), except in line 5, where it falls after the 7th syllable.

(*d*) No line has less or more than ten syllables.

The second passage is from *Macbeth* (Act i, Scene iii, ll. 127–42):

Two truths are told,

1. As happ|y pro|logues to | the swel|ling act|
2. Of the | imper|ial theme.|—I thank | you, gen|tlemen.—
3. This sup|erna|tural | solic | iting|
4. Cannot | be ill|, cannot | be good: | if ill, |
5. Why hath | it given | me ear|nest of | success,
6. Commen|cing in | a truth|? I am Thane | of Cawd|or:
7. If good, | why do | I yield | to that | suggest|ion
8. Whose hor|rid im|age doth | unfix | my hair
9. And make | my seat|ed heart | knock at | my ribs|,
10. Against | the use | of nat|ure? Pres|ent fears |
11. Are less | than hor|rible | imag|inings|:
12. My thought, | whose mur|der yet | is but | fantast|ical,
13. Shakes so | my sin|gle state | of man | that funct|ion
14. Is smoth|er'd in | surmise, | and noth|ing is |
    But what | is not. |

The basis of the passage is clearly the line of five iambic feet, yet every line contains some variation from the original pattern, and the general effect is incomparably more dramatic than that of the first passage.

(a) There are several examples of the foot of two unstressed syllables, the effect of which is to throw a stronger stress on important words. The following are examples:

Line 1, third foot.	Line 6, second foot.
Line 2, first foot.	Line 8, third foot.
Line 3, third foot, and perhaps fifth.	Line 11, third foot, and perhaps fifth.
Line 5, fourth foot.	Line 14, second foot.

(b) Several feet have the accent 'inverted' (i.e. strong weak, ´˘) and hence are 'trochees'. Examples are:

Line 4, first foot and third foot.	Line 7, second foot.
	Line 9, fourth foot.
Line 5, first foot.	

As a corollary to this point, it may be noticed that in a few feet the accent is (nearly) equal on both syllables, the feet being 'spondees'. Two possible examples are: line 4, 5th foot, and line 7, 1st foot. Some readers, however, may regard these feet as iambic. The 1st foot of line 13 appears to be a spondee.

(c) In lines 1, 2, 5, 6, 8, 9, and 14, the caesura or pause falls at or near the middle of the line (i.e. after the 4th, 5th, or 6th syllable), but in several of the lines it is nearer the beginning or the end than one would find in 'regular' verse. In lines 7 and 12 it comes after the 2nd syllable; in line 10, after the 7th; in line 13, after the 8th. In line 4 there are two caesuras, one after the 4th, one after the 8th syllable. In lines 3 and 11 the caesura is either very faintly marked, or non-existent.

(d) There are several examples of 'overflow' or 'enjambe-ment'; that is, the sense of a sentence or clause, instead of ending with the line, overflows into the next. Two clear examples of this are in lines 10 and 11, and in lines 13 and 14: any pause after line 10 or 13 is impossible. There is also little, if any, pause between lines 1 and 2, 3 and 4, 7 and 8.

(e) Several lines contain more than the regular number of ten syllables. In some lines (e.g. 6) an extra syllable occurs at the end of the line, making what is called a 'feminine' ending. In lines 2 and 12 there are *two* 'hypermetrical' syllables at the end. Elision, which is the running together of two vowels or syllables, accounts for extra syllables in some lines, viz. in line 2 where '-ial' in the 3rd foot counts as one syllable, and in line 6 where 'I am' also counts as one. In lines 7 and 13 the termination '-ion' is perhaps elided into a single syllable making a feminine ending, as in l. 6; and in line 5 'given' is pronounced 'giv'n' (by elision of the 'e').

The proportion of irregularities is thus much higher in the second passage than in the first; indeed, there are almost as many as verse will bear without becoming chaotic. The passage from *Macbeth* is a good example of the very dramatic and expressive verse which Shakespeare was writing towards the end of his 'tragic period'. In the late comedies, the freedom is carried one stage further, though it may be questioned whether there is any gain in *dramatic* quality. The almost complete absence of rhyme in *Macbeth* (except in the witch-

scenes and at the conclusion of scenes) agrees with what one
would expect in a work of Shakespeare's late middle period.

Note 1.—Attention has been drawn above (p. 182 § (e)) to two
lines of twelve syllables. The name for a line of six iambic
feet is Alexandrine. Several lines with two extra syllables
occur in *Macbeth* (e.g. I. iii. 129, I. iii. 139, III. i. 81, III. ii. 28,
III. vi. 30), but some of these lines are only *apparent* Alexandrines, that is, they are lines which, in spite of their twelve
syllables, do not contain six accents. The line

> My thought, whose murder yet is but fantastical
>
> (I. iii. 139)

is only an *apparent* Alexandrine, since the last two syllables
are both unaccented. On the other hand, it is difficult to see
how such a line as

> Be bright and jovial among your guests to-night
>
> (III. ii. 28)

can be scanned except as a *real* Alexandrine. It has been
proposed to slur the middle syllable of 'jovial' and the first
syllable of 'among', but the effect of

> Be bright and jovial 'mong your guests to-night

is unpleasantly huddled. A similar objection would apply to
the scansion of III. vi. 30,

> Is gone to pray the holy king, upon his aid

as

> Is gone to pray the holy king, 'pon 's aid,

though this has been proposed. We must conclude that
occasional *real* Alexandrines are among the irregularities in
the verse of *Macbeth*.

Note 2.—Attention has been drawn in the Notes to the
irregular metrical form of line 5 in Act I, Scene ii. *Macbeth*
contains other lines of this type, e.g. II. i. 51, IV. i. 122, IV. iii.
111. The effect of such lines is in accordance with the harsh
and abrupt style of large portions of the play.

APPENDIX IV

EXTRACTS FROM HOLINSHED

1. THE PART PLAYED BY DONWALD IN THE CONSPIRACY TO KILL KING DUFF

(see Introduction, pp. 11, 12. Cf. I. vii, II. iii, II. iv.)

AMONGEST them there were also certeine yoong gentlemen, right beautifull and goodlie personages, being neere of kin vnto Donwald capteine of the castell, and had beene persuaded to be partakers with the other rebels, more through the fraudulent counsell of diuerse wicked persons, than of their owne accord: wherevpon the foresaid Donwald lamenting their case, made earnest labor and sute to the king to haue begged their pardon; but hauing a plaine deniall, he conceiued such an inward malice towards the king (though he shewed it not outwardlie at the first), that the same continued still boiling in his stomach, and ceased not, till through setting on of his wife, and in reuenge of such vnthankefulnesse, hee found meanes to murther the king within the foresaid castell of Fores where he vsed to soiourne. For the king being in that countrie, was accustomed to lie most commonlie within the same castell, hauing a speciall trust in Donwald, as a man whom he neuer suspected.

But Donwald, not forgetting the reproch which his linage had susteined by the execution of those his kinsmen, whome the king for a spectacle to the people had caused to be hanged, could not but shew manifest tokens of great griefe at home amongst his familie: which his wife perceiuing, ceassed not to trauell with him, till she vnderstood what the cause was of his displeasure. Which at length when she had learned by his owne relation, she as one that bare no lesse malice in hir heart towards the king, for the like cause on hir behalfe, than hir husband did for his friends, counselled him (sith the king often-times vsed to lodge in his house without anie gard about him, other than the garrison of the castell, which was wholie at his commandement) to make him awaie, and shewed him the meanes wherby he might soonest accomplish it.

Donwald thus being the more kindled in wrath by the words

of his wife, determined to follow hir aduise in the execution of
so heinous an act. Whervpon deuising with himselfe for a
while, which way hee might best accomplish his curssed intent,
at length he gat opportunitie, and sped his purpose as fol-
loweth. It chanced that the king vpon the daie before he purposed to depart foorth of the castell, was long in his oratorie
at his praiers, and there continued till it was late in the night.
At the last, comming foorth, he called such afore him as had
faithfullie serued him in pursute and apprehension of the rebels,
and giuing them heartie thanks, he bestowed sundrie honorable
gifts amongst them, of the which number Donwald was one,
as he that had beene euer accounted a most faithfull seruant
to the king. . . .

Then Donwald, though he abhorred the act greatlie in his
heart, yet through instigation of his wife, hee called foure of
his seruants vnto him (whome he had made priuie to his wicked
intent before, and framed to his purpose with large gifts) and
now declaring vnto them, after what sort they should worke
the feat, they gladlie obeied his instructions, & speedilie going
about the murther, they enter the chamber (in which the king
laie) a little before cocks crow, where they secretlie cut his
throte as he lay sleeping. . . .

Donwald, about the time that the murther was in dooing,
got him amongst them that kept the watch, and so continued
in companie with them all the residue of the night. But in the
morning when the noise was raised in the kings chamber how
the king was slaine, his bodie conueied awaie, and the bed all
beraied with bloud; he with the watch ran thither, as though
he had knowne nothing of the matter, and breaking into the
chamber, and finding cakes of bloud in the bed, and on the
floore about the sides of it, he foorthwith slue the chamberleins,
as guiltie of that heinous murther, and then like a mad man
running to and fro, he ransacked euerie corner within the
castell, as though it had beene to haue seene if he might haue
found either the bodie, or anie of the murtherers hid in anie
priuie place; but at length comming to the posterne gate, and
finding it open, he burdened the chamberleins, whome he had
slaine, with all the fault, they hauing the keies of the gates
committed to their keeping all the night, and therefore it could

not be otherwise (said he) but that they were of counsell in the committing of that most detestable murther.

Finallie, such was his ouer earnest diligence in the seuere inquisition and triall of the offendors heerein, that some of the lords began to mislike the matter, and to smell foorth shrewd tokens, that he should not be altogither cleare himselfe. But for so much as they were in that countrie, where hee had the whole rule, what by reason of his friends and authoritie together, they doubted to vtter what they thought, till time and place should better serue therevnto, and heerevpon got them awaie euerie man to his home. For the space of six moneths togither, after this heinous murther thus committed, there appeered no sunne by day, nor moone by night in anie part of the realme, but still was the skie couered with continuall clouds, and sometimes suche outragious windes arose, with lightenings and tempests, that the people were in great feare of present destruction.

Monstrous sights also that were seene within the Scotish kingdome that yeere were these, horsses in Louthian, being of singular beautie and swiftnesse, did eate their owne flesh, and would in no wise taste anie other meate. . . . There was a sparhawke also strangled by an owle.

2. THE REIGN OF DUNCAN AND HIS MURDER BY MACBETH
(cf. i. ii, i. iii, i. vii, ii. ii, ii. iv)

The beginning of Duncans reigne was verie quiet and peaceable, without anie notable trouble; but after it was perceiued how negligent he was in punishing offendors, manie misruled persons tooke ocasion thereof to trouble the peace and quiet state of the common-wealth, by seditious commotions. . . .

Makdowald . . . making first a confederacie with his neerest friends and kinsmen, tooke vpon him to be chiefe capteine of all such rebels, as would stand against the king. . . . In a small time he had gotten togither a mightie power of men: for out of the westerne Isles there came vnto him a great multitude of people, offering themselues to assist him in that rebellious quarell, and out of Ireland in hope of the spoile came no small number of Kernes and Galloglasses, offering gladlie to serue vnder him, whither it should please him to lead them. . . .

Makbeth speaking much against the kings softnes, and ouer-much slackenesse in punishing offendors, whereby they had such time to assemble togither, he promised notwithstanding, if the charge were committed vnto him and vnto Banquho, so to order the matter, that the rebels should be shortly vanquished & quite put downe, and that not so much as one of them should be found to make resistance within the countrie.

And euen so it came to passe: for being sent foorth with a new power, at his entring into Lochquhaber, the fame of his comming put the enimies in such feare, that a great number of them stole secretlie awaie from their capteine Makdowald, who neuerthelesse inforced thereto, gaue battell vnto Makbeth, with the residue which remained with him: but being ouer-come, and fleeing for refuge into a castell (within the which his wife & children were inclosed) at length when he saw how he could neither defend the hold anie longer against his enimies, nor yet vpon surrender be suffered to depart with life saued, hee first slue his wife and children, and lastlie himselfe, least if he had yeelded simplie, he should haue beene executed in most cruell wise for an example to other. . . .

Thus was iustice and law restored againe to the old accustomed course, by the diligent means of Makbeth. Immediatlie wherevpon woord came that Sueno King of Norway was arriued in Fife with a puissant armie, to subdue the whole realme of Scotland. [Holinshed describes how this invasion was frustrated by the destruction of the hostile fleet.] Woord was brought that a new fleet of Danes was arriued at Kingcorne, sent thither by Canute king of England, in reuenge of his brother Suenos ouerthrow. To resist these enimies, which were alreadie landed, and busie in spoiling the countrie; Makbeth and Banquho were sent with the kings authoritie, who hauing with them a conuenient power, incountred the enimies slue part of them, and chased the other to their ships. They that escaped and got once to their ships, obteined of Makbeth for a great summe of gold, that such of their friends as were slaine at this last bickering, might be buried in saint Colmes Inch. . . .

A peace was also concluded at the same time betwixt the Danes and Scotishmen, ratified (as some haue written) in this wise: That from thenceafoorth the Danes should neuer come into Scotland to make anie warres against the Scots by anie maner of meanes. . . . Shortlie after happened a strange and vncouth woonder, which afterward was the cause of much trouble in the realme of Scotland, as ye shall after heare. It fortuned as Makbeth and Banquho iournied towards Fores, where the king then laie, they went sporting by the waie togither without other company, saue onelie themselues, passing thorough the woods and fields, when suddenlie in the middest of a laund, there met them three women in strange and wild apparell, resembling creatures of elder world, whome when they attentiuelie beheld, woondering much at the sight, the first of them spake and said; All haile Makbeth, thane of Glammis (for he had latelie entered into that dignitie and office by the death of his father Sinell). The second of them said; Haile Makbeth thane of Cawder. But the third said: All haile Makbeth that heereafter shalt be King of Scotland.

Then Banquho; What manner of women (saith he) are you, that seeme so little fauorable vnto me, whereas to my fellow heere, besides high offices, ye assigne also the kingdome, appointing foorth nothing for me at all? Yes (saith the first of them) we promise greater benefits vnto thee, than vnto him, for he shall reigne in deed, but with an vnluckie end: neither shall he leaue anie issue behind him to succeed in his place, where contrarilie thou in deed shalt not reigne at all, but of thee those shall be borne which shall gouern the Scotish kingdome by long order of continuall descent. Herewith the foresaid women vanished immediatlie out of their sight. This was reputed at the first but some vaine fantasticall illusion by Mackbeth and Banquho, insomuch that Banquho would call Mackbeth in iest, king of Scotland; and Mackbeth again would call him in sport likewise, the father of manie kings. But afterwards the common opinion was, that these women were either the weird sisters, that is (as ye would say) the goddesses of destinie, or else some nymphs or feiries, indued with knowledge of prophesie by their necromanticall science, bicause euerie thing came to passe as they had spoken. For shortlie after, the thane of Cawder being condemned at Fores of treason against the king committed; his lands, liuings, and offices were giuen of the kings liberalitie to Mackbeth.

The same night after, at supper, Banquho iested with him and said ; Now Mackbeth thou hast obteined those things which the two former sisters prophesied, there remaineth onelie for thee to purchase that which the third said should come to passe. Wherevpon Mackbeth reuoluing the thing in his mind, began euen to deuise how he might atteine to the kingdome; but yet he thought with himselue that he must tarie a time, which should aduance him thereto (by the diuine prouidence) as it had come to passe in his former preferment. . . .

The woords of the three weird sisters also (of whom before ye haue heard) greatlie incouraged him herevnto, speciallie his wife lay sore vpon him to attempt the thing, as she that was verie ambitious, burning in vnquenchable desire to beare the name of a queene. At length therefore, communicating his purposed intent with his trustie friends, amongst whom Banquho was the chiefest, vpon confidence of their promised aid, he slue the king at Enuerns, or (as some say) at Botgosuane, in the sixt yeare of his reigne. Then hauing a companie about him of such as he had made priuie to his enterprise, he caused himselfe to be proclamed king, and foorthwith went vnto Scone, where (by common consent) he receiued the inuesture of the kingdome according to the accustomed maner. The bodie of Duncane was first conueied vnto Elgine, & there buried in kinglie wise ; but afterwards it was remoued and conueied vnto Colmekill, and there laid in a sepulture amongst his predecessors, in the yeare after the birth of our Sauiour, 1046.

3. THE MURDER OF BANQUO AND THE ESCAPE OF FLEANCE (cf. iii. i, iii. iii)

Makbeth (governed) the realme for the space of ten years in equall iustice. But this was but a counterfet zeale of equitie shewed by him, partlie against his naturall inclination to purchase thereby the fauour of the people. Shortlie after, he began to shew what he was, in stead of equitie practising crueltie. . . . The woords also of the three weird sisters, would not out of his mind, which as they promised him the kingdome, so likewise did they promise it at the same time vnto the posteritie of Banquho. . . .

It chanced yet by the benefit of the darke night, that though

the father were slaine, the sonne yet by the helpe of almightie
God reseruing him to better fortune, escaped that danger: and
afterwards hauing some inkeling (by the admonition of some
friends which he had in the court) how his life was sought no
lesse than his fathers, who was slaine not by chancemedlie (as
by the handling of the matter Makbeth woould haue had it to
appeare) but euen vpon a prepensed deuise: wherevpon to
auoid further perill he fled into Wales.

4. MACBETH AND MACDUFF (cf. IV. i, IV. ii)

Neither could [Macbeth] afterwards abide to looke vpon the
said Makduffe, either for that he thought his puissance ouer great;
either else for that he had learned of certeine wizzards, in whose
words he put great confidence . . . that he ought to take heed
of Makduffe, who in time to come should seeke to destroie him.

And suerlie herevpon had he put Makduffe to death, but
that a certeine witch, whome hee had in great trust, had told
that he should neuer be slaine with man borne of anie woman,
nor vanquished till the wood of Bernane came to the castell of
Dunsinane. . . . This vaine hope caused him to doo manie
outragious things, to the greeuous oppression of his subiects.
At length Makduffe, to auoid perill of life, purposed with himselfe to pass into England, to procure Malcolme Cammore to
claime the crowne of Scotland. But this was not so secretlie
deuised by Makduffe, but that Makbeth had knowledge giuen
him thereof. . . . For Makbeth had in euerie noble mans house
one slie fellow or other in fee with him, to reueale all that was
said or doone within the same, by which slight he oppressed
the most part of the nobles of his realme.

Immediatlie then, being aduertised whereabout Makduffe
went, he came hastily with a great power into Fife, and foorthwith besieged the castell where Makduffe dwelled, trusting to
haue found him therein. They that kept the house, without
anie resistance opened the gates, and suffered him to enter,
mistrusting none euill. But neuerthelesse Makbeth most
cruellie caused the wife and children of Makduffe, with all other
whom he found in that castell, to be slaine. . . . Makduffe was
alreadie escaped out of danger, and gotten into England vnto
Malcolme Cammore.

5. MACDUFF AND MALCOLM IN ENGLAND [throughout Act iv, Scene iii. 1–139, Shakespeare follows Holinshed as closely as he does in this short passage] (cf. iv. iii. 102–37)

Then said Makduffe: This yet is the woorst of all, and there I leaue thee, and therefore saie; Oh ye vnhappie and miserable Scotishmen, which are thus scourged with so manie and sundrie calamities, ech one aboue other! Ye haue one curssed and wicked tyrant that now reigneth ouer you, without anie right or title, oppressing you with his most bloudie crueltie. This other that hath the right to the crowne, is so replet with the inconstant and manifest vices of Englishmen, that he is nothing woorthie to inioy it: for by his owne confession he is not onelie auaritious, and giuen to vnsatiable lust, but so false a traitor withall, that no trust is to be had vnto anie woord he speaketh. Adieu Scotland, for now I account my selfe a banished man for euer, without comfort or consolation: and with those woords the brackish teares trickled downe his cheekes verie abundantlie.

At the last, when he was readie to depart, Malcolme tooke him by the sleeue, and said: Be of good comfort Makduffe, for I haue none of these vices before remembered, but haue iested with thee in this manner, onelie to prooue thy mind: for diuerse times heeretofore hath Makbeth sought by this manner of meanes to bring me into his hands, but the more slow I haue shewed my selfe to condescend to thy motion and request, the more diligence shall I vse in accomplishing the same.

6. THE VICTORY OF MALCOLM AND MACDUFF OVER MACBETH (cf. Act v, Scene vii).

[Macduff addresses Macbeth]: Now shall thine insatiable crueltie have an end, for I am euer he that thy wizzards have told thee of, who was neuer borne of my mother, but ripped out of her wombe: therewithall he stept vnto him, and slue him in the place. Then cutting his head from his shoulders, he set it vpon a pole, and brought it vnto Malcolme. . . . Malcolme Cammore thus recouering the relme (as ye haue heard) by support of king Edward, in the 16 yeere of the same Edwards reigne, he was crowned at Scone the 25 day of Aprill, in the yeere of our Lord 1057.